Praise for See What Love Can Do

"The journey Mary shares with us in *See What Love Can Do* tracks a loving path from deep tragedy to healing through a process she creatively calls 'Infinite Generosity.' As someone who has received a horrific phone call that brought me to my knees, I can unfortunately relate to Mary's story and her initial sense of grief, horror, guilt, and confusion. The healing process Mary shares and the lessons she has learned provide a deeply thoughtful and compassionate glimpse for the reader of the four states of Infinite Generosity. The book gives an enlightening new perspective on self-care and inner peace. Thank you for sharing this, Mary."

—**Alex Freytag,** Creator of ProfitWorks®, Expert EOS Implementer®, and Author of *Vision Works, Profit Works,* and *Stretch Not Snap*

"Mary gets real and vulnerable and takes us on an unexpected journey from tragedy to wisdom. She asks us to take a hard look at our lives and gives us tools to live more expansively. Thank you, Mary! We all need to hear this message again and again."

—**Sara B. Stern,** Expert EOS Implementer® at EOS Worldwide, Business Coach, Host of *The Experiment,* and *Family Business Fanatic*

"This isn't a book about surviving tragedy. It's about the radical choice to write a new story when others are writing one for you. Mary's vulnerability is staggering, and her framework for moving through pain is something I'll carry with me. Read this if you've ever been stuck between bitterness and grace."

—**Ginger Zumaeta,** Founder and CEO of Motive3, Author, Emmy and Muse Award winner

"Mary shares her beautiful story of how her love of swimming turned into a successful business, then tragedy. Through her tragedy, the teacher became the student, and it brought her back to her life's work of learning to 'Float'... for her to surrender her life to Infinite Generosity and back to her faith. If you're struggling with a life event where you feel you're sinking and can't breathe, this book is for you to learn Mary's insights on Giving, Receiving, Observing, and Floating to experience true peace and love."

—**Don Maranca,** President of JDSM Enterprises and Expert EOS Implementer®

"Mary Reilly-Magee has lived the truths in this book long before she ever put them on the page. I know this because, as her coach, I had the privilege of witnessing her reclaim her voice and live the truths in this book long before she ever put them on the page. This is not theory; it is the fruit of a woman who walked through suffering with God and chose love instead of fear. Her realization that 'nothing outside of me defines me' is the freedom every entrepreneur longs for. *See What Love Can Do* is the beautiful fruit of Mary's return to faith—a journey that creates healing, peace, and courage, one holy choice at a time."

—**Mike Kotsis,** Creator of Freedom Coaching

"This is not a book you simply read; it's a book you are held by. In *See What Love Can Do,* Mary Reilly-Magee offers a story told with extraordinary honesty, humility, and grace. Through unimaginable loss, she invites us into a deeper understanding of love, not as a feeling, but as a daily, intentional choice. A choice to give, to receive, and to stay open when it would be easier to close ourselves off. Mary doesn't rush us past pain or offer platitudes. Instead, she walks beside us through grief, responsibility, faith, and healing, showing us what it looks like to live with integrity when life falls apart. Her concept of Infinite Generosity is both profound and practical. This framework gently reshapes how we relate to ourselves, to others, and to the hardest chapters of our lives. This book is for anyone who has faced a moment that changed everything, and for those who want to meet life with more compassion, courage, and love. Mary's voice is steady, brave, and deeply human. Reading this book feels like being reminded that even in our most broken moments, love is still available to us. With it, we are capable of transforming everything."

—**Samantha Kris,** Executive Speaker Coach and Certified Reinvention Practitioner

"*See What Love Can Do* is a courageous and deeply compassionate book, one that never looks away from the weight of tragedy, while gently inviting the possibility of healing alongside it. Mary writes with honesty, humility, and grace, offering a powerful framework for navigating loss without minimizing it. Her concept of Infinite Generosity helped me reflect more intentionally on giving, receiving, and allowing support during life's hardest moments. This book is a profound guide for anyone seeking meaning, connection, and a way forward after unimaginable pain."

—**Miren Oca,** Founder and CEO of Ocaquatics Swim School; Founder of Ripples of Impact Non-profit

"*See What Love Can Do* reminds us that generosity is a necessary aspect of life. Much like water is necessary for learning to swim, generosity is necessary for the attainment of peace. Mary provides a substantial yet accessible approach to cultivating generosity in the smallest and largest ways."

—**Kevin Moore,** Principal at i•financial

"*See What Love Can Do* is for anyone who has experienced traumatic pain, such as major surgery, a traffic accident, the loss of a loved one, or the loss of a business. Getting through any traumatic event requires help: a surgeon, a physical therapist, or your family members. You are suddenly plunged from being the helper to someone who needs help to accomplish the most basic functions of life. It is not just about allowing others to help; it is about assisting and enabling them to be the very best version of themselves. No one goes through life without experiencing trauma. It can be physical, emotional, or financial. Our bodies and souls react the same to trauma and need the same help and healing. *See What Love Can Do* is a roadmap for both those suffering and those giving care. It is a GPS for those pain-filled, difficult days."

> —**George Block,** Owner of Island Fitness and Vice-President of World Swimming Coaches Association

"Mary's insights in this book have come from the deepest part of her, and in that, she has created a transformational and totally unique pathway for being in the space of LOVE with generosity. She's disrupted, reframed, and deepened my relationship with generosity that will no longer leave me quietly drained, but instead has led us on a pathway to expansive, infinite heart-based generosity."

> —**Jill Young,** Creator of Coaching Magic, Expert EOS Implementer®, Author of the Advantage Series, and Podcast Host

"*See What Love Can Do* puts into words what I've kept to myself: how hard it is to accept help and how worn out I get from giving too much. Mary's Infinite Generosity framework—moving easily between Giving, Receiving, Observing, and Floating—helps me stop overthinking and shows me a better way. These are lessons learned the hard way by someone who's been through real tragedy, and they give a clear understanding of how love actually works."

—**Jim Spiers,** President of Stop Drowning Now; CEO of Main Street Academies and SwimJim, Inc.

"I work with leaders every day who struggle to ask for help. Mary's framework on giving, receiving, and floating gave them—and me—permission to stop keeping score and start trusting the flow of generosity. Watching Mary transform her tragedy into wisdom for all of us has been remarkable. *See What Love Can Do* is honest, practical, and hopeful. If you're exhausted from over-giving or uncomfortable receiving, this book is for you."

—**Beth Fahey,** Expert EOS Implementer®, Co-author of *Rollout: Get Your Entire Team Running on EOS to Achieve Your Vision*, Host of *Bad Boss Confessional* podcast

"Mary's courageous and personal vulnerability, starting with a broken heart, makes this book a profound standout in a world of impersonal business books. Her concept of Infinite Generosity proves that the flow of love is the most impactful strategy for life. I highly suggest this book for any leader looking to gain permission to stop clinging to control and learn to simply float."

—**Tom Cuthbert,** CEO Coach and Vistage Master Chair

"A gut punch and a love punch masterfully delivered. Mary has beautifully turned the raw, unfiltered reality of tragedy into a love and grace-filled bank of wisdom to help anyone not just survive a tragedy but to truly thrive beyond it."

—**Justin Maust,** Entrepreneur, Keynote Speaker, and Expert EOS Implementer®

"Raw and relatable, bold and biblical, this book is incredibly practical for everyday life. The concept of Infinite Generosity engages the intellect, spirit, and emotions, revealing the beauty of receiving and offering a thoughtful perspective on giving with love rather than giving for love."

—**Russell A. Reyes,** Founder and CEO of Pericos Mexican Restaurant and President of Panchito's Mexican Restaurant

"I am a lifelong learner and on a continual quest to discover confirmations of spiritual truths that exist in my everyday world. I began reading this book with preconceived notions of what love and generosity are, shaped by how I experience them in my daily life. I was completely blown away by Mary's novel concept of the 'four states of being,' which compelled me to examine—often uncomfortably—how consciously I choose, or fail to choose, my own state of being. As a friend, wife, boss, doctor, mother, sister, daughter, and servant of God, I am continually sharing my time, energy, and experience with those around me—often to my own detriment. *See What Love Can Do* helped me take inventory of the many ways I believed I was being generous, while gently challenging me to recognize that allowing others to help me is also a profound form of generosity. This shift in perspective allowed me to replenish a deeply depleted well within myself and opened new pathways for giving that I never imagined could so beautifully multiply my impact in the world. Mary does a remarkable job guiding readers through the fog of trauma—a space we can all recognize as a moment when everything changed, and we longed for a community that could truly see and understand us. Regardless of belief system, this book offers compelling evidence of a universal truth: we are not meant to live this life alone. *See What Love Can Do* is brilliant and will fill and move your soul into action."

—**Dr. Melody Zamora,** Founder and CEO of Zam Dental

"Being vulnerable enough to open one's soul is not easy; walking out pain is hard. What Mary has masterfully shown us with Infinite Generosity is that giving and receiving can make us whole. She's given us a very special message with action to give and receive for the sake of love, peace, and soulful freedom."

—**CJ DuBe',** Speaker, Best-Selling Author, Expert EOS Implementer®, Former Global Community Leader at EOS Worldwide LLC.

SEE WHAT LOVE CAN DO

Moving from Pain to Peace through Infinite Generosity

Mary Reilly-Magee

Story BUILDERS PRESS

See What Love Can Do: Moving from Pain to Peace through Infinite Generosity

Copyright © 2026 Mary Reilly-Magee

No part of this book may be reproduced or transmitted in any form or by any means, electronic or mechanical, including photocopying and recording, or by any information storage or retrieval system, except as may be expressly permitted by the Copyright Act of 1976 or in writing from the publisher. Requests for permission should be addressed to storybuilderspress@gmail.com

Published by StoryBuilders Press

ISBN: Hardcover: 979-8-89833-052-1

ISBN: Paperback: 979-8-89833-053-8

ISBN: eBook: 979-8-89833-054-5

For Mitchell—May this book honor your memory and create a positive impact far beyond anything we could have imagined.

For Love to Swim School—May this story honor the greatness created by the many people who contributed to its success and lasting impact.

For my husband, Don, and my children, Reilly and Donovan—who sacrificed so much for my dream.

Contents

Chapter 1: When You Have Nothing Left to Give   1
Chapter 2: We Live through Different States   25
Chapter 3: Giving   45
Chapter 4: Receiving   63
Chapter 5: Observing   81
Chapter 6: Floating   99
Chapter 7: Go with the Flow   123
"If," by Rudyard Kipling   143
Acknowledgements   149
About the Author   157
Resources   159
Notes   163

CHAPTER ONE

When You Have Nothing Left to Give

Life can become unrecognizable in the time it takes to answer the phone.

If you've never had a phone call like that—the kind that splits your world in two—I hope you never do. I mean that with all of my heart. I hope your phone never rings with news that makes your knees buckle; I hope you never have to ask someone to repeat themselves because your brain simply refuses to process their words, because accepting what they're saying would mean accepting the unacceptable.

On Saturday, February 10, 2018, I attended the US Swim School Association spring conference as a member and a presenter. I spoke to a group of swim school business owners and their staffs about teaching breath control to learn-to-swim students across all skill levels—from those who are terrified of the water to those developing fluid, rhythmic freestyles. Then, I had dinner with friends, brainstorming ways to offer our support and advice to one who was struggling personally and professionally.

And then my phone rang.

The call I received was about a child. One of our little preschoolers named Mitchell. The voice on the other end of the phone proceeded to explain that he drowned in one of the pools I owned—in a place meant to be as safe as it could be, a happy gathering spot where families came to learn, play, and build confidence in the water. His parents were taking advantage of our Date Night event for the first time, trusting that their child was in good hands.

But the incomprehensible happened.

And just like that, my life split into a before and an after.

Some of you already know what I'm talking about. You've stood where I stood—in that eerie, suspended, stunned space where time bends and the air feels different. It's like a door slams shut in your head and you can feel in your body the finality of its permanence.

Nothing will ever be the same.

The worst part in the early days and even weeks after the accident was waking up not remembering momentarily—and then, excruciatingly, remembering.

This happened.

It's true.

And nothing you do can change it; though my brain worked on it endlessly, rolling back the tape in my mind again and again, unable to accept the reality of this tragedy. Unable to understand the fact of it because of the absolute needlessness of it.

All you had to do was watch the water.
Watch the water.
Watch the kids in the water.
Keep them safe and help them have fun.

The thing about these life-changing calls is that they don't just change one moment of your life. They can change the entire trajectory of your life. One minute, I was a successful, award-winning business owner with three locations and nearly a hundred staff members—a leader in the learn-to-swim business community and water safety education, a valued member of my local business community. The next, I was the woman whose swim school was connected to an unthinkable tragedy—struggling to breathe inside the wreckage of a family's worst nightmare while bearing the weight of accountability for what happened.

What's so disorienting is how ordinary the moment before the call was. I wasn't bracing for bad news. I wasn't sitting by the phone waiting. I was just having a fun dinner with my best friends who happen to share a passion for teaching people to swim well. We were happy and grateful to be together. And then the phone rang.

There's no handbook for how to exist after a call like that. It's simultaneously an out-of-body experience and an inescapable, visceral imprisonment in your own skin. Blame and guilt come at you from the outside. Grief and anger churn on the inside. Shame whispers that you deserve this. Indignation argues back that you don't. Every thought becomes a referendum on who you are and what you've done and haven't done.

I remember half-seriously asking my therapist for a shot that would make the pain go away. Oh man, I longed for that shot—something, anything, to numb what felt crushing and, at times, unsurvivable. There's no easy solution for how to stand back up when the ground has been ripped out from under you. But here's what I can tell you from the other side: you cannot do it alone.

If you've already had your own phone call—if you're living in the after—I see you. I'm standing here, hand outstretched, from my own patch of uneven ground, still learning to walk steady.

And if your phone hasn't rung yet, I hope with my whole heart it never does.

But if it does, I want you to remember this: you are not alone. There will be hands to hold you. All you have to do is let them give you their support and love. Let yourself receive.

Why Do We Resist Help?

Sometimes life falls apart so completely that the trauma short-circuits our ability to think clearly or make decisions. In those moments, all we can do is surrender to the help that shows up—not because we're wise enough to accept it, but because we're too shattered to refuse it.

That phone call was like that for me.

But there are other times—the majority of times, really—when we're struggling but still functioning. We could use help. We probably need it. But we're capable of saying no, so we do. We deflect. We minimize. We insist we're fine when we're barely holding it together.

I've had plenty of those moments too.

During the times when we are coherent enough to choose whether or not we can receive help, a word other than yes or no can make its way into the conversation, just below the surface. That word is "can't." It comes hand-in-hand with the feeling of resistance. It's as if the very moment we most need others, we become the most determined to prove that we can do it alone. It's not logical. It's not helpful.

And yet, we do it anyway.

Why is it so hard to let people help us when we're hurting or overwhelmed? Why, when we're at our most fragile, do we suddenly try to insist we're fine when we're anything but?

I understand the instinct to fold in on yourself, to curl up in a ball and disappear. I know how tempting it is to refuse every offer of help because admitting you need it feels like admitting defeat—like confessing you're somehow weaker than you're supposed to be.

But let me tell you something I learned: resisting help doesn't make you strong.

It just makes you alone.

When tragedy struck, there were times when I felt that initial pull to self-protect. To hole up inside my pain, where no one could see just how shattered I was. There's something about suffering that makes us think we should do it alone, as if pain is a private shame we're supposed to carry in silence.

Maybe it's pride. Maybe it's fear. Maybe it's the deep-seated belief that accepting help somehow diminishes us, makes us weak, or places a burden on those who are offering. But here's what actually happens when we resist: *crushing isolation.* Bitterness. Amplified suffering. The very weight we're trying to carry alone presses down even harder.

If we're being brutally honest, it seems the resistance is all ego. It's the part of us that says, *I can do this by myself. I don't need anyone. I'm fine.* It's the voice that tells us we'll be a burden if we let people in—that our grief, our pain, our messiness will be too much for them.

That voice is a liar.

When we block people from helping us, we're not protecting them—we're isolating ourselves. We're building a wall around our suffering and locking ourselves inside. We'll end up alone with our mental gymnastics, cycling through the same painful thoughts with no one to help us see a way out.

The truth is, when you're hurting, your perspective is limited by your pain, your exhaustion, and the sheer weight of what you're carrying. You need other people to help you see what you can't. You need their objectivity, compassion, and steady hands when yours are shaking too hard to hold on to anything.

And here's the twist—receiving help isn't just for you. It's for the people who love you, too.

Think about it. When someone you care about is suffering, what's the worst feeling in the world?

Helplessness, right?

It's that gnawing, powerless ache of knowing they're in pain and not knowing how you can make them feel better. When you say yes to help—even if it's just letting someone bring you a meal or sit beside you in silence—you're offering them a gift. You're giving them a way to show their love, to ease their own feelings of helplessness, to feel like they've done something when there's so little anyone can do.

It's letting yourself receive, even when it feels awkward or undeserved, because you understand, deep down, that generosity isn't a one-way street. It's an infinite loop, anchored in love. When you let someone care for you, you're giving them something precious: ***a role to play in your healing***.

Infinite Generosity

We've been taught to recognize generosity in one direction: giving. But true generosity, the kind I've come to call Infinite Generosity, moves both ways. It lives within all of us as a virtue, not just in saints or philanthropists.

Picture an infinity symbol, continuously flowing. One side is giving: your time, resources, wisdom, care. The other is receiving: allowing someone else to offer those same gifts to you. The symbol works because it moves. There's breath in the exchange, a dynamic flow that aligns us with something deeper—a universal truth that's built into the fabric of human connection.

We are meant to take turns.

Some of us give instinctively. We're the first to offer a meal, raise a hand, fix what's broken. Others have learned to receive, through experience or necessity. They've leaned on others and been vulnerable. Most of us shift back and forth depending on the season of life or the situation we're in.

The shifting we experience isn't weakness; it's wisdom.

Our typical idea of balance, where giving and receiving are perfectly weighed and measured, doesn't apply here. Instead, consider a fluid movement involving awareness and participation.

When we give, we make space for someone else to receive. When we receive, we make space for someone else to give. Rather than being transactional, it's relational. The infinity loop isn't a circle because life isn't always symmetrical. Sometimes we give more. Sometimes we need more. We're not striving for balance. We're striving for flow. Yet most of us struggle with this. Giving gets celebrated. Receiving feels complicated, especially for those accustomed to being the strong, dependable one.

But receiving with grace is its own form of generosity. When we let someone show up for us, we're not just taking—we're creating an opportunity for someone else to give. We're connecting with our own humility, accepting support without diminishing ourselves. There's trust involved here: that my submission to your help won't make me less than. And faith: that we can accept without strings, reprisals, or judgment. Receiving says, "You matter, too." That's a gift.

Of course, most of us have been shaped by stories that make this hard. Maybe we learned that asking for help is a burden, that needing something makes us weak, that our value depends on how much we produce or serve. Those beliefs keep us stuck, clinging to one side of the infinity loop and resisting the other.

When that happens, our flow slows. Movement stagnates. We give until we're empty, or receive without learning to give back. We isolate, perform, and pretend we're fine.

But what if we could step out of that pattern? What if we began to see Infinite Generosity not as something to earn or prove, but as something to return to again and again?

When it comes to facing our own generosity infinity loop, we're not working on a trendy new personal development project or a moral obligation. Rather than getting it right, we're trying to see ourselves inside the bigger story.

Infinite Generosity is relational at its core. It connects us to ourselves, to each other, and to something sacred and unseen. It's the invisible thread that holds us together and reminds us we don't have to do this life alone.

When we step into the current of the Infinite Generosity infinity loop, something shifts. We can stop white-knuckling our way through. We soften, notice, trust. We ask different questions. Not "What do I owe?" or "What do I deserve?" but, "Where am I in the flow today?" and "What's being asked of me right now—to give or to receive?"

This practice changes us. It helps us pay attention to where our energy is going, where we need refilling, and how we participate in a cycle that nourishes everyone. It invites us to be honest about our tendencies, our defaults, and the places where we resist connection. And it gives us language to name where we are, without shame.

Infinite Generosity isn't rigid. It adjusts to our lives. It holds space for seasons of strength and seasons of need. It honors the full spectrum of the human experience. Because all of us will have moments when we hold someone else up, and moments when we are the ones being held. Neither is more valuable. Both are holy.

When Life Knocks You Down

In the wake of the tragedy, I was overwhelmed by an outpouring of love from an incredible network of people in my life. These were the people who had allowed me to contribute to our profession, build deep relationships, and grow alongside them in community. We had helped each other through the ups and downs of building learn-to-swim businesses, planting seeds and forming relationships without any thought of reciprocation. It was about our entrepreneurial peer community and building a tribe of like-minded people.

Because I understood the value of peer advisory groups, I joined The Alternative Board (TAB) in 2009 and remained until 2021, and I joined the Entrepreneurs' Organization (EO) in 2012, where I'm still a member today. I've been part of the US Swim School Association since 2003—the community where I met my best friends and later served as a board member, president, and vice president–elect.

When the earth cracked open beneath my feet, my tribe showed up before my brain could comprehend how much I needed them. In the fog of my shock and disbelief, I couldn't make decisions—and they knew it. They swooped in and took action.

My best friend, Rose, was with me from the very first second, literally sitting at the table when the call came in. She immediately grabbed her laptop and searched for flights home while I sat frozen, trying to comprehend what I'd just heard. On day two of the conference we were attending, as I was arriving back in San Antonio, she walked up to the podium and made the announcement every aquatics professional dreads: a child had drowned at one of my swim schools.

I can only imagine how that news landed in that room—the collective gasp, the horror, the instinctive empathy mixed with relief that it wasn't their school. From that moment, my swim school community rallied around me, helping me craft a press release when I could barely form coherent thoughts.

When my head said, *I can't let you do that for me,* somewhere in the blur of people, logistics, and grief, my heart heard a still, strong voice—clear and firm.

Say yes.

I knew that voice was right. So I did something I wasn't used to doing. I said yes. I made a commitment to say yes.

Yes to every offer of help, large or small, practical or emotional. It was my first effort to move myself from one side of the generosity infinity loop to the other, though I didn't know it at the time.

There were calls, visits, emails, and offers of help—more than I could process. But Rose stayed at the center of it all. She didn't just show up once and disappear. She wove herself into my grief, staying with me emotionally and sometimes physically, through every impossible step that followed.

In the weeks after we reopened our location, Rose flew to Texas from her home in California to walk through the building with me. She was there when I met with families. She held me up mentally as I faced my clients, my community, and all of those who were grieving around me.

Rose could see what I was doing—pulling everyone's grief onto my own shoulders. The families' grief. My staff's grief. The community's grief. My family's grief. It was crushing, threatening to collapse me under its impossible burden.

But in the midst of it all, I had this tribe surrounding me.

They showed up day after day, even as they navigated their own emotions—their own vulnerability in their businesses, their own questions, their own sickness about this totally preventable drowning death. They were grieving too, shaken by the fragility of the work we all do and the unthinkable reality that our worst fear could come true. Yet they didn't turn away. They leaned in, held me up, and reminded me I didn't have to carry it alone.

And every Saturday morning for the next five years, Rose called. She listened to me say the same things a thousand different ways—listened when I was lost in the fog, overwhelmed by the enormity of what had happened, in agony over the loss of this mother's son, maligned by people who didn't know the truth, and lied about so viciously it made me question humanity itself. People who had never met me, never stepped into my schools, never asked a single question—they created elaborate narratives about who I was, what I'd done, what kind of person I had to be that I would let this happen. They turned me into a villain in a story they invented, and there was nothing I could do to stop it.

Rose listened when I couldn't make sense of anything or find my footing, when the ground beneath me felt like it was constantly shifting. She listened when I needed to tell the story over and over, each retelling a desperate attempt to reshape the narrative, to find some version where it hurt less, where I could breathe again. I circled back to the same questions, the same anger, the same grief, trying to piece together how everything had shattered so completely. And she never grew tired of it. She never rushed me or told me it was time to move on. It was central to my healing and my sanity—having someone who would bear witness to my pain without judgment, without needing me to be okay before I was ready. She kept listening.

We still have those Saturday morning conversations, a sacred space where we see and hear each other, grounding each other in grace and objectivity. I love having that time set aside for the two of us.

It wasn't just Rose who showed up for me during that time.

There was this incredible group of brilliant, successful swim school owners, my Girl's Trip friends, so called because we took trips together to visit and learn from other swim school businesses, putting our heads together on our common challenges and opportunities for improvement. They made sure that I stayed connected to their love and support. One of my biggest fears was losing them—my best friends in both business and life. They continually welcomed me into their circle and refused to let me drift away.

When I went on the first girl's trip after the accident, it was uncharted territory for all of us. I was no longer a swim school business owner. I was someone else—someone yet to be determined, still taking shape in the wreckage. I'll never forget the moment Rose pulled out a black tank top. "Look," she said, "I got this for all of our workout buddies." On the back, it read: "Most often, it is not the workout that gets us out of bed in the morning. It is the friendships and unspoken bonds of those counting on us to show up." When she turned it around, I saw the words across the front: *Mary's Tribe*.

It was the best kind of gut punch. I gasped and started sobbing right there. To be stood up for, supported in such a tangible, physical way—it was the most beautiful gift I've ever received. And it became the seed for this book.

The whole group wore those shirts as they stood with me in my grief. They wore them every year after that trip, sending me pictures and reminding me that I belonged, that I was held, that I was one of them.

It's hard to describe what that kind of love does for a person. It's the opposite of shunning—it's an intentional surrounding, a deliberate wrapping up in care. It's arms around you, holding you upright when you feel like you might disappear into the darkness or crumble to the ground, unable to put the pieces back together. Even all these years later, the generosity of that shirt and what it represented makes my eyes sting with gratitude. I'll never forget it.

There are so many different instances of this outpouring of love that I could fill this book with stories alone. Let me share a few that still take my breath away:

My beautiful friend, Miren Oca, working through the US Swim School Association, organized a Google Sheet. Every week for an entire year, people signed up to send something to me, my family, my staff, and all three of my locations. Those generous acts of kindness kept me going when I felt like I was going to collapse under the weight of it all. Notes, gifts, food, and inspirational messages of support arrived. Banners for the walls appeared, created by swim school teams across the country, telling us that the work we were doing mattered, encouraging us to keep going. They saw us in our pain, and they kept showing up.

Somewhere in that blur, a friend sent the biggest bag of peanut M&M's I've ever seen, along with a whoopee cushion and bathroom jokes, a beautiful attempt to coax a smile out of the darkness. There were little stones etched with *Let all you do be in love. Corinthians 16:14*, one of which I still reach for even now when I need to remember. There was a trip to Tampa with Micha Seal and Miren where, again, I was too dull to know it was a rescue mission.

Then there was the quilt. My colleague Casie Shore organized it, and Tammy Schoen hand-delivered it—a quilt made of T-shirts from swim schools across the country. It's a living map of encouragement, with each square representing someone who cared enough to stitch themselves into my life during my darkest time. They told me to use it to wrap myself in their support, which, of course, I did, again and again.

It wasn't just gifts or packages. It was people physically showing up.

On that first Monday, after the accident became the biggest news story of the weekend in San Antonio, I sat at my desk, staring blankly out the window of my corporate office, unsure how to even begin. I watched as cars started pulling into the parking lot—one, then another, then another. Friends from my peer advisory groups, from EO, and from the Alternative Board walked through my door without being asked. They sat with me in the heavy silence, helped me sort through the impossible decisions I couldn't make alone, and simply stayed when there was nothing left to say.

Weeks later, the visits continued. Sometimes, they'd see me on the phone through my office window and pause—not interrupting, just acknowledging. A gentle wave. Heart hands pressed against the glass. A small, encouraging smile. Silent messages that said: *We're here. We see you. You're not alone.*

Pat, my "Catholic brother," sent me a note of support and love that arrived exactly when I thought I couldn't go on any longer—one of those moments when the timing felt divinely orchestrated.

For my birthday, four days after the fatal drowning, my EO Forum gave me a gold necklace with a small, round plate charm engraved with a single word: *Strength*. I added a cross charm beside it and have clutched it through countless tough conversations and challenging situations since then, a tangible reminder of who I am and Whose I am.

Even when the press came, my tribe shielded me. They met the reporters at their vans, climbed in to talk with them, humanizing the story and reminding them that my pain mattered too. They helped the reporters see who I was—not a headline, but a person. A grieving person trying to survive an unthinkable tragedy in a business created to prevent such a thing.

It was a miraculous, beautiful gift: the gift of not being alone.

One of my first instincts when life knocked me flat (and maybe yours, too, when tragedy strikes) was to ask *why*. The questions came fast and relentless, each one pulling me into a spiral of blame and second-guessing.

But before I could spiral too far down that rabbit hole, the voice returned.

No. DO NOT ask why.

I stopped. Confused. Angry, even. How could I not ask why?

But then I understood: There is no good answer. No logic or explanation could ever make any part of what happened that day okay. No amount of analysis would bring that child back or undo his parents' agony. The why wasn't mine to solve. My work was to say yes to the help, the love, the arms reaching out toward me.

That yes didn't come easily, especially when the fog of trauma began to lift and reality came into sharper focus. Everything in me wanted to withdraw, to disappear into the darkness. That's what shame does: it convinces you that you deserve to be alone with the pain, that you've forfeited your right to comfort or connection.

But I wasn't the only one living through this.

One of my biggest wake-up calls was watching my husband navigate his own devastation. He was engulfed in sadness, grief, and anger—emotions he had no outlet for because everyone's focus was on me. He had willingly climbed aboard this learn-to-swim business ride with me years earlier, supporting my dreams and helping turn them into reality. He gave endlessly to help me build what I'd envisioned—weekends and evenings spent fixing broken equipment, or family dinners postponed for staff emergencies. Somewhere along the way, he stopped calling it my dream and started calling it ours. There were countless sacrifices we made together to create and grow this life. And now, in an instant, because of someone else's mistake, it was all gone. Not just the business, but the future we'd built together, brick by brick, sacrifice by sacrifice.

My husband—my sweet, steady husband—was terrified he was going to lose me. Not to the tragedy itself, but to the aftermath. To the grief that was swallowing me whole. When I lifted my head, I could see it written all over him: In his eyes when he thought I wasn't looking, in the tension that never left his shoulders, in the way he watched me like I might shatter into a thousand pieces or simply fade away. The sadness pooling in his expression. The helplessness in his silence. The fear he tried to hide. The anger at his own powerlessness to fix this, to fix me, to make any of it better.

He had stood beside me for years, believing in me fiercely. He had been my steady ground, my constant encourager, my safe place to land. And now, the weight of my grief was pulling me under—and threatening to drag him down into the darkness with me.

I realized that I had to try for him. I had to fight for my own healing. Not just for me, but for us. For the life we'd built together. For the man who refused to let go of my hand even when I wanted to let go of everything.

I'll be honest—there were days when it felt impossible. The anger, the shame, the relentless question of whether I could have done something, anything, to prevent this. The trial in my head on a constant loop: What part of this did I truly own? What part did I personally play in this tragedy?

It all felt like an open wound, raw and exposed, refusing to heal. There were moments when it felt like something was pressing directly on the wound—a social media post calling me a murderer, a vicious Yelp review from someone who'd never met me or been a customer at our school, online comments that felt like a digital mob armed with lies and invented details—like someone was driving their fist straight into that wound, leaving me gasping and paralyzed with fresh agony.

Then I'd remember the voice: *Say yes.*

That's the secret no one tells you about receiving: It isn't passive. It's giving someone else the gift of showing up, letting them be a part of your pain, your survival, and your eventual healing.

I know how hard it is. I know because I lived it. But when you say yes, when you let people in, when you allow yourself to need and to be cared for, you're not just saving yourself. You're reminding the people who love you that they matter, too. That their generosity has a place in your life.

Receiving is an act of generosity. One that takes humility, courage, and trust. And it's one of the greatest gifts you'll ever give to yourself and those who love you.

Step into the Loop

I hope you're starting to see the concept of a generosity infinity loop not as some abstract idea, but as something real—something already present in your life, whether you've noticed it before or not. The truth is, this isn't just a theory or a nice metaphor. It's happening all around you, all the time. You now have the opportunity to start seeing it and to start noticing how you engage with it.

Let's start small. I invite you to begin looking for evidence of the loop in your own life.

Where do you see generosity flowing?

Who is showing up to give?

Where have you been the one offering a hand, a listening ear, a meal, or a ride?

Who's been there to offer those things to you, and how did you respond?

Did you say yes?

Did you wave them off?

Did you accept with a smile while trying to hide those uncomfortable feelings?

All of that is information. All of it helps you understand your own personal dance with giving and receiving.

Here's where I hope you get a little curious, because this is not about judgment. It's about awareness. When you pause in a moment of decision—when someone offers to help or you feel an impulse to give—ask yourself, *What's the generous thing to choose here?*

Think of it as being generous toward the situation as a whole, and toward yourself as well as the other person. What if you decided in your head what you wanted to do and then paused for one more step?

What if you dropped into your heart and asked the same question: *What's the generous thing to choose here?*

I can almost guarantee that your heart will give you a slightly different answer. Your head might say, *Don't bother her with this.* But your heart might say, *She'd love to help.* Your head might say, *It's too much to ask.* Your heart might say, *You deserve care, too.* That's the tension you're navigating—the pull between independence and interdependence, between protection and connection.

Now, let's talk about where you're stuck, because we all have places where the loop has slowed to a crawl or is completely jammed up. Maybe you're giving so much at work, at home, and in your community that you've forgotten how to receive. Maybe you're in a season where you desperately need help, but pride, fear, or habit keep you from asking for it. Or maybe you're somewhere in between, not quite aware of how your relationship with giving and receiving is shaping your experience of life.

Whatever your situation, I invite you to try an experiment. Apply generosity to those stuck places.

Ask yourself:

What would it look like to be generous with myself right now?

What if I extended generosity to the other people involved in a particular situation?

What if I were generous toward the situation itself, trusting that there's more happening here than I can see?

How could I be generous with my ego, maybe letting go of my need to control or prove something?

What would it mean to be generous with my reputation, caring less about how I'm perceived and more about what's real and true?

Generosity, when applied broadly, opens up new avenues of possibility. It invites solutions, connections, and insights that defensiveness and self-sufficiency could never touch. It doesn't mean that you suddenly become a doormat. It means you trust the loop, and that when you open your hands, something new can come in.

If you're ready for something practical, try the following:

Challenge yourself to accept help or kindness this week without deflecting, downplaying, or minimizing it. Say thank you and notice how it feels.

Was it uncomfortable? Was it unexpectedly sweet? Did it change how you saw the giver or yourself?

Find one small, meaningful way to give today. It doesn't have to be grand. Offer your time, attention, or kindness.

See how it feels. Notice how it impacts the person receiving it and how it impacts you.

Be random and play with it.

These little moments are how you step back into the flow, start clearing the blockages, and remind yourself that you were never meant to live this life alone.

Infinite Generosity is waiting. All you have to do is step into it, one act of giving and one act of receiving at a time.

CHAPTER TWO

We Live through Different States

Most of us understand generosity as something that flows from us toward someone else. We have more, so we give. We're capable, so we help. We're strong, so we carry others. It's a linear transaction: giver and receiver, helper and helped, strong and weak.

But in my journey through trauma and toward healing, I've experienced firsthand a truth that transforms everything: We all need both sides of that flow—the giving and receiving—to truly live a peaceful, fulfilling life. The loop must be complete. The energy must flow both ways.

When we block one side of that infinity symbol, when we refuse to receive with the same grace we give, we cut ourselves off from the very source that sustains us.

Life presents endless challenges to all of us—loss, failure, betrayal, tragedy, moments that shake us to our core. The question isn't whether these things will happen. The question is: Who are you going to be when they do? And how do you want to feel about your choices when you look back at what you've survived?

For a long time, I felt like I couldn't share the most painful part of my story. There were moments when I convinced myself it was too dangerous, that speaking openly could invite more attacks, more judgment, more pain. I worried I could do more harm by putting the truth out there—harm to others, harm to myself, harm to the fragile healing I was desperately trying to protect. So I stayed quiet. I stayed small. I let fear and hurt make my decisions.

But I've learned over time that the connection that comes from sharing our stories—even the messy, heartbreaking, complicated ones—is more powerful than any protection isolation can offer. Hiding kept me safe, but it also kept me stuck. I've put in the hard work to reclaim my voice, to stand in my truth without shame, and to trust that vulnerability is not weakness but courage.

And now, I'm ready to share what I've learned—not because I have all the answers, but because I've walked through the darkness and found my way back to the light. And if my story can help even one person feel less alone in their darkness, then every hard-won lesson, every painful step forward, will have been worth it—as cliché as that sounds.

With one phone call, I was forced to stop being the helper and become the helped. When I had no choice but to let myself be loved and held and carried by others, in that breaking open, I discovered the true meaning of generosity. It wasn't what I thought it was.

This is your invitation to rethink generosity as something far more transformative than random acts of kindness or charitable giving. It's a conscious practice, a daily discipline, a way of moving through the world that creates deep fulfillment in your life. When you start to embrace both sides of generosity—when you learn to receive as openly and graciously as you give—something profound happens. The exhaustion lifts. The resentment fades. Life feels lighter, more connected, more whole. You stop running on empty and start flowing with abundance. This is the gift that was born from my greatest pain. And now, I'm offering it to you.

The Four States

Instead of seeing generosity as something we bestow upon others, we can recognize it as four states that we step into—always as a participant in something bigger than ourselves. Generosity isn't a fixed point. It's a living spectrum, always shifting and always available. Most of us fall into one of four primary states, depending on the season, situation, or day: Giving, Receiving, Observing, and Floating.

The chart below can help you identify where you are right now. Take your time with these possibilities. The goal isn't to box yourself in. It's to get curious about what resonates with you.

Before you continue, pause for just a moment. Not to judge or fix, but to notice. Where do you land in this moment? What comes naturally? What feels difficult? Tune in to your body. What are you feeling, and where? What is it telling you?

There's no wrong place to be, only an honest one.

That's the beauty of Infinite Generosity. It starts with truth, and it moves with love. Love in action, love in presence, and love in return. More than what you do, consider who you are becoming—and how you choose to move with others, yourself, and grace.

States of Being Along Infinite Generosity Loops	
Giving (Imagine an infinity symbol with a larger loop on the giving side.)	Receiving (Imagine an infinity loop with a larger loop on the receiving side.)
Observing (Imagine an infinity symbol that is almost completely flat.)	Floating (Imagine a perfectly normal infinity symbol.)

Giving. You are constantly pouring out. You show up for others, carry responsibilities, and offer your time, energy, expertise, money, or emotional presence. You are busy. This feels purposeful and energizing, until it becomes exhausting because you rarely let yourself receive in return. This state often feels familiar to those who feel most comfortable when they're needed.

Receiving. You are taking in support, help, love, or care from others or even from yourself. You might be recovering from something or learning to let others show up for you. This state can feel tender, vulnerable, uncomfortable—especially if you're not used to being the one in need.

Observing. You've stepped back from the flow of the infinity loop altogether. You are watching more than you are participating. Life may have slowed down, or you have pulled away to process, reflect, or rest. This state helps you gain clarity, but it can become isolating if you linger in it too long.

Floating. Giving and receiving feel natural and fluid. Ease replaces the feeling of holding back or overextending. You respond to life with a lightness that doesn't come from trying harder—it comes from trusting more. This state is beautiful, but it isn't permanent. And that's okay.

A Moment of Surrender

While writing this chapter, more than seven years after the accident, I found myself falling right back into a familiar pattern of suffering.

The foundation the family created to honor their son had its Swim Safety bill back in front of the Texas legislature for the third time. Mitchell's mom, April, ran for a seat on the city council, using swim school business regulation and her son's drowning death at my facility as qualification for the position and a foundation of her campaign.

All the old emotions flooded back. My mind raced, reliving the pain and sorrow for the thousandth time. I put myself back on trial, mentally relitigating "the case" against me, bristling at inaccuracies, misrepresentations, and exaggerations like I was fighting for my life. Mentally defending my former business, my team, and myself from old accusations of carelessness, recklessness, cheapness, or money hunger. I found myself rehearsing the same internal monologue I've returned to again and again over the years.

As if disproving those accusations enough would make them stop.

But the truth is, it won't.

Of course they won't. That's how the family is surviving it. That's how any of us would.

And so I had a choice to make. Again.

Am I going to get back on this rollercoaster? The one that rolls through my inbox every time the legislature is in session, every time that version of what happened makes its rounds? Am I going to strap myself into every twist of her grief and every drop of her blame? Or can I choose something else?

Can I let this mom grieve the way she wants to grieve? Even if that grief looks like misinformation and misunderstanding to me?

What is the generous thing to choose here?

What does it mean to love someone who tells a version of your shared tragedy that feels like a betrayal of the truth?

What does it mean to love and honor myself in that same space?

The truth is, that mom—April—trusted us at Love to Swim School. That trust didn't appear out of nowhere; it was built, one swim class after another, over nine months. Nine months of watching her boys grow more confident in the water. Nine months of waving at familiar faces on the pool deck. Nine months of conversations with coaches and quiet nods of appreciation and pride in the progress.

When she signed them up for Date Night, there was no reason not to trust us. And I had no reason not to trust us either. We had offered Date Night for twelve years without incident. We had the training, credentials, and systems in place, tested and true.

But we also had a failure. There was a breakdown in protocol, a cascade of thinking errors and assumptions that created an environment tragically conducive to a terrible accident.

Mitchell died in a place designed to prevent that very thing. And I will never stop holding the truth of that paradox with reverence. In order to teach people how to swim, we have to provide the very thing that could take their lives. The risk is inherent. All we can do is mitigate it.

As a mother, I have to stand with the mom who lost her son. Not because I agree with her version of events, but because I understand the depth of her loss. I can't let myself get distracted by the misinformation and hyperbole. I can't lose sight of the real tragedy. Her son died.

I stand with her in disgust, disdain, anger, and grief. Not in the details of the story she tells, but in the heartache that drives her to tell it. That's the only path forward for me, the only one that leaves room for love and honor.

So what does that look like?

It means I no longer fight for control of her narrative. Not in my spirit, my inbox, or my kitchen while rehashing it with people who love me. I choose not to get on that ride. I don't buy that ticket. I don't even go to the park.

Instead, I send her love. Energetically, spiritually, and intentionally. I send her mercy, grace, forgiveness, healing, and peace. These are all the things I want from her, her family, her community. What if I allow her to grieve her way, even and especially when it costs me something?

That's **Giving** in its purest form.

It's not the glamorous kind. It's not accompanied by applause or recognition. It's the hidden generosity of the soul. The kind that honors another person's pain even when it clashes with your own.

But to give that way, I've had to **Receive** first. Receive grace, mercy, healing, moments of peace. I've been reminded that my worth isn't found in my perfection or my reputation. That I will stumble and fall when life blindsides me, when my inner voice turns cruel and engulfs me in guilt, grief, anger, and sadness. That I am not defined by the worst thing that happened to me. I am defined by God alone, and I intend to live in love—His love.

I know who I am, and when I slow down, upon reflection, connection, and intention, I know I can come back to a place of love and generosity.

Observing is the bridge. That's what helps me pause before I react. It's what allows me to witness her pain without absorbing it as my own. Observing gives me the breath I need to choose compassion over self-protection or defense.

And sometimes, honestly, I just have to **Float**. I have to surrender what I can't fix. I have to rest in the misery and the mystery of it all—that both of us are telling the truth of our grief, even when our stories don't match.

The ability to choose love didn't come to me overnight. It has taken intentional choices to work toward wholeness again, toward oneness with God, to realign with Him. I've worked with therapists and coaches, and even participated in healing plant medicine experiences to find my way back. And guess what? I'm still a work in progress. That's okay.

Love is the only thing wide enough to hold us both. So I do my best to choose love. I choose honor. I choose to be generous with my energy, even when I feel depleted. I choose to let go of the fight and simply float in the deep end of grace and mercy, where answers don't come easily, but peace is possible.

The Three Rules of Infinite Generosity

These three simple rules helped me grow. They're not rigid laws—they're guideposts, gentle reminders to return to when you feel disoriented or unsure of where you are in the flow of giving and receiving.

I didn't discover them all at once. They revealed themselves slowly, through trial and error, joy, and discomfort. Each one helped me get unstuck when I didn't even realize I was stuck. They helped me move when I was scared, soften when I was defensive, and remember that Infinite Generosity isn't a destination—it's a series of states we move through.

These rules help you notice what's happening beneath the surface. They strengthen self-awareness instead of demanding perfection. Take what resonates. Set aside what doesn't. Let them be invitations to explore as you learn about Infinite Generosity.

RULE 1: Don't Let Your Values Slow Your Flow

Our values are the quiet truths that help us make decisions, define our purpose, and navigate our lives. They are essential. But sometimes, the very values that once guided us can become so ingrained and unquestioned over time that they start to restrict us rather than free us.

Consider hard work. Maybe you grew up believing that success comes from effort—that you earn every achievement through long hours, self-sacrifice, and grit. You became dependable, productive, and proud. But what happens when life offers you something good that comes easily? Does the achievement feel less worthy because it didn't cost you enough? Do you receive it with gratitude, or do you question whether you deserve it? Do you feel guilty when you rest?

These are all signs that the value of hard work has stopped flowing and started hardening. It's no longer a guide. It's becoming a rule, and rules don't bend.

Or take independence. You take pride in managing your own life, making your own decisions, never being a burden. There is power in that. But there's also isolation. When independence turns into self-preservation, you build walls around yourself out of fear. You tell yourself you're fine, even when you long for connection. You stay in the Observing state longer than you need to because it feels safer than re-entering the infinity loop.

Even kindness can bind us when we confuse it with being agreeable. If you grew up believing that kindness means never causing discomfort or conflict, you avoid hard conversations or constantly adjust to other people's needs at the expense of your own. Over time, that sort of generosity becomes heavy. You are giving, but it's more about keeping the peace than sharing your heart.

And humility—we're told it's important to stay humble no matter what we achieve. But humility often gets confused with smallness. In the Receiving state, you need humility to accept love and care without feeling weak or ashamed. But if you internalize humility as staying quiet, asking for less, or never taking up space, it stops being a strength. It becomes a cage.

This is how the flow of Infinite Generosity can get stuck: We let our most cherished values solidify. Instead of gripping them tightly or abandoning them completely, we need to hold them lightly, let them evolve, and stay curious about how they show up in our lives.

A value should breathe. It should guide you toward love, not fear. So when something that once felt life-giving starts to feel constricting, that's your invitation to pause and ask, "Is this value still flowing with me, or have I built my identity around it so tightly that I've stopped moving?" When you find the answer, don't rush to fix it. Just notice. That's where movement begins again.

RULE 2: *You're Not Going to Be 100 Percent of Any of These*

One of the most liberating things I've learned about Infinite Generosity is that you don't have to master it. You don't have to live all the time in a state that's perfectly balanced between giving and receiving, or keep score to make sure you are doing your fair share. That's not how this works.

The important part is paying attention. Where do you feel most at home? Where do you feel stretched too thin? What makes your heart soar, and what feels forced? Maybe you are a generous giver who struggles to let anyone return the favor. Or maybe you are a gracious receiver who isn't sure how to offer something back. Maybe you have felt all of these things at different points in your life. I know I have.

And here's the beauty of it: There is no finish line. No perfect formula to memorize. It's about recognizing where you are, being honest with yourself about where you want to be, and making small adjustments along the way. The flow of giving and receiving isn't rigid. It's alive, moving, and personal.

You may recognize yourself in one of the four states: Giving, Receiving, Observing, or Floating, but you are not only one of them. You are all of them at different times, in different ways. And that is exactly as it should be.

Some seasons of your life will be marked by extraordinary giving. Others will ask you to receive deeply, even when you'd rather not. Some chapters will require solitude and observation, while others feel so peaceful that you'll wonder if you've finally cracked the code.

And then things will shift again, because life is never static, and neither are you. Did you know that the summary of all of Buddha's lessons is that everything changes? I just learned that, and it certainly tracks.

The danger is in thinking you have failed or are doing it "wrong" because you are not living in the ideal state. The infinity loop of Infinite Generosity is designed to move, and that movement is what keeps your relationships honest, your energy aligned, and your heart open. Instead of asking yourself, "Which one am I supposed to be?" try asking, "Which one feels most true right now? Which one feels uncomfortable but necessary? Which one is calling for me to soften or stretch?"

You get to meet yourself, over and over again, in all the different places you land. That's how you can find fulfillment with Infinite Generosity. Let yourself be a work in progress.

RULE 3: *You Must Have Faith*

Over time, I've discovered that Infinite Generosity works best when we're in motion. The infinity loop between giving and receiving isn't a line you follow or a phase you complete. It's a rhythm, a movement, a living, breathing cycle. And it doesn't matter where you are on it. What matters is that you continue to move.

When you get stuck in one place too long, everything starts to feel off. You get tired, bitter, frustrated, self-righteous, or embarrassed. You stop seeing yourself clearly. You start noticing little signals from the people around you—eyes that look away, energy that subtly withdraws, conversations that end with a hint of awkwardness. None of it is because you're broken, selfish, or too much. It's because your movement along the loop of Infinite Generosity has paused.

That feeling of stuckness is the cue, and the only way to respond is with faith. I mean that literally. Faith is the thing that lets you move. It lets you float.

When I created an adult learn-to-swim program, what struck me was that most people weren't there to learn freestyle. They were there to overcome fear. And I'm talking about deep, primal, full-body terror.

I learned quickly that I needed to be vigilant during these sessions. Some people would step into the shallow end and immediately spiral into total panic. Their breathing would go shallow and rapid. Their eyes would lock onto the wall, the ladder, anything solid. I could see the exact moment fear took over—their rational mind shut down, and something ancient kicked in.

The fear of drowning is so powerful that it overrides the very behaviors necessary to prevent it. They'd thrash when they needed to relax. Hold their breath when they needed to exhale. Fight the water when they needed to trust it. Terror doesn't listen to logic. It just screams: *Get out. Now.*

And I was asking them to trust me.

It's one thing to teach a stroke. It's another to hold someone's fear in your hands and make sure you don't break their trust. One mistake on my part could solidify their fears or make them worse. I had to carry a do-no-harm mindset while also nudging them forward. There's a sacred tension in that: honoring the emotion without indulging it, calling someone forward without pushing them too fast. It required both of us to show up with a mix of courage, patience, and faith.

These were grown adults. They were strong, intelligent, capable people with jobs and mortgages. But the second they considered putting their face in and picking their feet up off the bottom of the pool, their breath shortened, their eyes got wide, and underneath it all, they believed one thing: *I am a rock. If I let go, I will sink straight to the bottom.*

But that wasn't true, physically or psychologically. Their bodies were made to float. It didn't matter how many times I told them, though; it only clicked when they experienced it for themselves. I was there for support, and this process was incremental. Their hands were on my shoulders as they tested their buoyancy. Then their hands moved to mine. Then their hands hovered above mine, ready to catch them if panic struck.

So the very first thing I did was get them comfortable putting their face in the water. Not just dipping their chin—actually submerging. Mouth, nose, eyes. The whole face. For some, this alone took several lessons. We'd start with just their lips touching the surface, exhaling slowly in a hum to learn to hear and feel the breathing, building trust one millimeter at a time.

Next came breath control so they didn't panic when water crept up their nostrils. They'd practice exhaling through their nose and mouth—steady streams of bubbles rising to the surface. Then we'd work on rhythmic breathing, the kind that becomes automatic, almost meditative. Finally they'd learn to delay the exhale, to hold that breath and trust their lungs wouldn't betray them. Then came floating. The real test.

Incrementally, step by step, I would ask them to curl up in a little ball, hold their breath, pick up their feet and tuck their knees into their chests, "Just let go," I'd say. And every single time, they would sink a little. That initial drop always caught them off guard—their eyes would flash with panic, their bodies would tense. But I'd remind them, "Stay with it. Don't fight. Just wait."

And then, the water would lift them. Not because they fought for it, or flailed, or performed. Simply because that's what water does: It buoys you. It finds your edges and holds them.

They would rock forward and back. They would wobble a little, testing the limits of their trust. If they could stay with it—if they could resist the urge to grab for the wall or plant their feet—they'd reach stillness. A perfect, weightless suspension.

Then they would look up at me, wide-eyed, faces breaking into disbelief and wonder, as though they had witnessed a miracle. Some would laugh. Some would cry. That shift from terror to trust was everything.

The movement along the infinity loop of Infinite Generosity asks the same thing of us. We need to loosen our grip on the identity we have clung to for so long. We must lift our feet. And that can be terrifying. It's terrifying to stop relying on brute strength. It's terrifying to stop justifying our weakness. It's terrifying to move when standing still has become so familiar, so safe, so known.

Please hear me when I say *you were made to float*. Infinite Generosity was designed to carry you with ease through the different states of being. It can feel a little wobbly. You might sink a little before you lift back up. But you are not a rock, and you are not stuck. You are meant to be in motion, even when you don't know how you'll get moving again.

That's where faith comes in. I'm not asking you for blind optimism or to believe everything will turn out okay if you work hard enough. Faith is knowing that the water holds. The infinity loop flows, even when you're scared. Especially when you're scared.

When we stay too long on one side of the loop, we start mistaking it for identity. We become a role to play. Those roles might have served us at one point, but they are not the whole of who we are. No state of being is permanent. It's more like a dance.

The moment you start to feel stagnant, your energy is off, relationships are strained, or the joy is dulled, that's your cue. Not a failure. Just a nudge that it might be time to pick up your feet.

Let yourself flow again. Trust it. Trust yourself and the people who love you. Trust that you don't have to grip life so hard. That if you allow it, the water will buoy you. That's the kind of faith I'm talking about—the kind that makes movement feel natural instead of shameful or dramatic.

We are not meant to stay in one state of being forever. The strength is in knowing when it's time to move and believing you will be okay on the other side. You don't have to know where the movement will take you. Just trust that it will carry you to a place where you feel more at peace.

So if you're stuck and beginning to wonder what's wrong with you, remember that nothing's wrong. You are overdue for movement. And movement requires faith. Faith that Infinite Generosity flows continuously. Faith that letting go doesn't mean losing yourself. Faith that you were made for this.

Take a breath. Put your face in. Pick up your feet.

Diving Deeper into the States of Being

Here we are, at the edge of understanding. If you are still unsure where you fit along the loop of Infinite Generosity and the states of being, that is completely normal.

You don't have to nail down your state like a pin on a map. That's not the point. The point is to notice when you are clinging, coasting, hiding, or wide open. This understanding is the beginning of your intentional movement. If you are wondering whether it's okay to still be figuring it all out, let me assure you, I'm still learning right along with you. I don't say that to be humble. I say it to be honest.

I am on this journey, too. I have my own crisis-of-faith moments, and because I want to live in Love, I have to slow down and reset myself. And that's okay.

Some days we give freely. On other days, we need to receive with open hands. Sometimes we step back to observe without judgment, and at our best, we float. Not above it all, but in it. Fully suspended in the present, held by something larger than ourselves.

In each of the coming chapters, I will offer what I've discovered about each state of being. First, we'll dive deeper into what it means to live in the Giving state—not because it's the best place to be, but because it's the starting point for so many of us. You'll learn how to live generously in every sense of the word.

CHAPTER THREE

Giving

Let me tell you more about my friend, Rose. She's the 2024 Citizen of the Year in Davis, California, an honor that barely scratches the surface of her long-term commitment to service. She's one of the most awarded people I know. If there's a humanitarian recognition, a guiding light tribute, or community spotlight to be given, chances are it's been handed to Rose. And if her town has something called SwimAmerica Day, it's not just because she runs a successful business by that name. It's because of the way she lives.

Rose is the kind of woman whose heart breaks at the tragic death of a local police officer and then creates a massive community fundraiser called "Touch a Truck" to honor her memory. She hosts. She serves. She's been the Chamber of Commerce president, Rotary Club president, and a board member of Thriving Pink. She buys local, is working to make her business a Certified B Corp, and she gives time away at her family condo in Tahoe for her friends' rest and enjoyment.

She sits by your side when you're hurting. She checks in. She calls and reaches out. She'll jump into action or stay completely still if you just need her presence as she quietly listens. She has a servant's heart, not because she's trying to be nice or liked, but because it genuinely brings her joy. It's who she is. It's how she's wired.

I remember the days when that joy got tangled up with resentment. I could see it in those big brown eyes of hers, fringed with eyelashes that could sell mascara if they weren't so busy narrowing in on quiet disappointment. She'd give and give and give, and it would gnaw at her that rarely did anyone say thank you. No Boss's Day card. No acknowledgment. She'd get in her car and cry. It would wreck her. All she wanted was to be seen.

I think that's when I began to understand the heartbreak of the unrecognized Giver. We talk about burnout, but we don't talk about that slow erosion that happens when someone gives so much and starts to feel invisible in return.

For you to understand Rose, I need to share what she's carried.

Early in their marriage, which was late in life, when both of them were in their fifties, her husband was hit during a cycling ride on California's Highway 101. He had no ID on him. When the police called, he was a John Doe in the ICU—intubated, on a ventilator, barely recognizable. Broken back. Broken neck. Broken leg. Serious head injury. He lost his sight in one eye.

It was their second major health scare, and this one rewrote their future.

When I got the call, I remember saying, "I'll be on the next plane." To which she replied, "Wait. Krysten's here (her daughter). Let me assess the situation." She's that kind of strong and steady. But don't mistake strength for easy acceptance. She mourns what could have been: their travel dreams, and the freedom they imagined. But she still shows up daily, with her eyes and heart wide open.

That's giving.

John can't drive on the highway anymore. It's hard for him to carry and lift their luggage, and his physical limitations can take a toll on Rose sometimes. In those moments, I want her to be more generous with the many people who love her and John, and simply ask for help.

Rose, I must point out, rarely asks for help. She's in her sixties, but climbs ladders and hauls supplies from her car like a twenty-five-year-old, often because she doesn't want to be a burden. I've watched her struggle, and I've felt frustration rise in me. *It pisses me off*, honestly. I want her to learn to receive. She's slowly getting there, more open now than before. But it's been a journey.

Obviously, Rose lives primarily in the Giving state of being. Not because she's perfect, but because she's human. She's walked the long road from depletion to discernment.

From martyrdom to mutuality. From giving for love to giving with love.

If you're in this state, this chapter is for you, especially if you're exhausted.

When Giving Becomes a Stereotype

When we're living in the Giving state, it feels good to show up for others, lend a hand, and pour ourselves into causes and people we care about. But when we lean too far into giving, we can end up feeling depleted, unappreciated, or resentful. It's a delicate balance, and none of us gets it right all the time.

To help make sense of the most common patterns, I've given these archetypes some playful names. They are not meant to box anyone in. Remember, no one is ever 100 percent one way. But chances are, you'll recognize some of these types in the people around you. And if you're open and honest with yourself, I bet you'll start to see yourself here, too. As you read these descriptions, think about who comes to mind. More importantly, pay attention to which ones makes you wince a little—because it hits too close to home. That's part of understanding where you are right now.

Suffering Martyr. You've likely experienced this type before. The "yes" people who believe that selfless suffering is the only way to prove their worth. They'll move mountains for everyone around them, often while dramatically sighing under the weight of it all. Their calendar is always packed, and they wear their exhaustion like a badge of honor. They'll never, ever turn down an opportunity to help, or an opportunity to let you know just how much they are sacrificing. Their inner monologue sounds something like, It's fine, I'll just do it myself. Again.

People Pleaser. You can spot People Pleasers easily—they are the ones buzzing around like busy worker bees. They are at every bake sale, charity run, and community event. They don't seem to understand the meaning of personal downtime or a good night's sleep. You won't hear them admit they're overwhelmed. In their minds, being helpful is the only way to feel worthy. Deep down, they just want to feel appreciated, but they rarely stand still long enough to let anyone show it.

Obligated Contributor. The Obligated Contributor is always doing the right thing—with just a hint of resentment if you watch them closely. They help you move your couch or babysit your dog because family helps family, right? You see them trying to smile through their frustration, but you can't miss that side-eye or those tense shoulders. They genuinely want to give from a place of joy, but they can't shake the feeling of being burdened by duty. Their giving isn't always rooted in generosity. It's still kind, but the clouded intention dims the joy that a purely generous act *could bring.*

Scorekeeping Supporter. This giver has an internal scoreboard continuously running. They are acutely aware of who owes what and who they're even with. They are happy to help as long as they know it's a fair trade. You will hear them say things like, "Well, I did this for you last week, so . . ." They want to give selflessly but are often stuck calculating whether they're giving too much or too little. Their fear of being taken advantage of overshadows the beauty of their generosity.

Understanding Yourself in This State

One of the ways I've come to understand this state is by paying attention to the values that drive it. The giver isn't just someone who offers help. They are animated by internal principles, deep motivations that point toward love, dignity, and justice for others. But, like anything powerful, these values have two sides. They can bring out the very best in us, and they can also take a toll when we are not paying attention.

Let's start with empathy. Givers feel things deeply. They don't just notice someone else's pain; they feel it in their own body. That level of emotional intelligence is a gift. It creates a connection. People feel seen and cared for. But it can also become emotionally exhausting. When you are constantly attuned to others' needs, it's hard to locate your own. And when your empathy turns into overfunctioning—carrying feelings that don't belong to you—it starts to drain instead of energize.

Compassion takes empathy a step further. Givers don't just feel; they want to act. They want to relieve suffering themselves. That's beautiful and powerful. But I've learned (sometimes the hard way) that excessive compassion can morph into enabling. Doing for someone what they are meant to do for themselves not only depletes the giver—it also unintentionally keeps the other person from growing.

And then there's **generosity**, which is one of the most radiant parts of this state. A giver doesn't withhold. They take joy in sharing: knowledge, time, food, money, presence. They want to give. But this value can leave us vulnerable, too. Some people take advantage of that openness. Some simply aren't capable of receiving reciprocally. And when that happens, the giver can be left feeling used, unappreciated, or confused about what generosity even means.

Integrity and responsibility round out the value system that often defines a giver. These values are especially close to my heart. For me, doing the right thing matters. It's not about appearances; it's about me being able to look myself in the eye with a clear conscience. And that sense of integrity has served me well, especially in hard leadership moments.

At Love to Swim School, we weren't just teaching swimming lessons. We were developing people. Over the course of twenty years, we hired hundreds of young adults between the ages of eighteen and twenty-four and trained them not just in swim instruction, but in leadership, communication, time management, and personal growth. We called it Love University—Love U, for short. It was a people-development company disguised as a swim school.

We did everything we knew how to do to develop our people. We held mandatory monthly in-service training meetings. We trained for specific safety and teaching scenarios. We developed and drilled our processes and procedures and practiced them again and again. We gave our people, largely college students, a place to grow, contribute, and lead. And I carried all of that with a deep sense of personal responsibility. It's how I'm built. I am a teacher, a coach, and an entrepreneur. Putting the tools in our team members' toolbox to keep students safe and provide an outstanding service was the only way to make the extraordinary business I sought to create.

But ultimately, all of it didn't matter. A preschooler still drowned because a couple of people didn't do what they'd been trained to do. Because complacency crept in. And as a giver whose core values include integrity and responsibility, that gutted me.

The dark side of integrity is inflexibility. It can turn into an "I have to" way of life. I *have* to do this. I *can't* say no. I *must* fix this. But that's not actually integrity. That's guilt masquerading as virtue.

So, how do you know when you are in the Giving state?

You'll notice that you're energized by helping others, but depleted when your giving isn't acknowledged or when the outcomes don't reflect your intentions. You might struggle to say no, even when it costs you more than you can afford to give. You might feel personally responsible for making things right, especially when you care deeply about the people involved. You'll feel both the satisfaction of showing up and the aching loneliness of wondering if anyone sees what it's costing you.

When you're in the Giving state, it's important to honor your values without letting them consume you. Giving should come from fullness, not emptiness. If this is where you find yourself, ask, "Am I giving from love or guilt? From overflow or obligation?" That's how you begin to understand yourself in this state. Not by judging it, but by witnessing it with compassion, just like you do for everyone else.

Tom's Story

On my quest for healing and wholeness, I have entertained and experimented with a lot of different paths to peace. Recently, I went to a three-day plant medicine retreat in the mountains. Twelve of us gathered, doing deep, courageous work—each person open to whatever was ready to surface. It was the kind of experience that leaves you equal parts broken open and astounded by the beauty of it all. And right in the middle of it was one of our facilitators; we'll call him Tom.

Tom was remarkable. Ever-present and steady. He anticipated our needs before we could voice them—blanket when the shivers came, water before our mouths went dry, a hand on the shoulder when the tears started. He talked each of us through our journeys with such gentleness and clarity; it was like he had a sixth sense for where to apply compassion and where to encourage a deeper surrender. He gave freely. We got to witness pure, grounded generosity—the kind that leaves you feeling safe enough to be completely undone.

And then, on the last integration day, when it was his turn to share, he said something that caught in my chest.

He talked about his anxiety around money. He shared about how hard it was to support his wife and child at the level he wanted. His deep fear was that his wife was disappointed with the life they were living.

This man, who had given so much, started to unravel in front of us. You could feel the weight of his shame in the room, along with his belief that his generosity only counted if it came without any need of his own.

When we started to offer our acknowledgment and support, it was like his whole body resisted. Not just mentally—but physically. His shoulders pulled back. His jaw tightened. He couldn't imagine letting us help.

We dug into it with him, gently and respectfully. And what we uncovered at the root was this: weakness and worth. Somewhere along the way, Tom had internalized the idea that accepting help meant that he had failed. That if he needed support, it meant he was weak. That to receive was to admit that he was not enough.

I asked if I could share something with him, and he nodded.

"Tom, generosity is an infinity loop. It's not a straight line. You're not meant to stay at one end forever. You gave us so much these past three days—the kind of giving that opens hearts and creates space for transformation. And now, it would make us so happy to support you in a way that meets you where you are. Because you supported us so beautifully."

Something softened in him, just a little. You could see it in his eyes. That little flicker of a new possibility: *Maybe I'm not weak for needing help. Maybe receiving is a way of honoring the people who love me.*

I think about that moment often, especially when I talk with people who are deep in the Giving state. Because most of us—especially entrepreneurs, in my experience—don't ask for help. At all. Or if we do, it's a last resort. And even when help is offered, we rarely accept it.

We think our value is wrapped in how much we can do for others. We mistake constant giving for strength. And what we don't see (and what Tom almost missed) is that receiving is not weakness or failure. It's what connects us to each other, this pulse of giving and receiving. Here, in the possibility of this mutuality, we get to meet each other most humbly and truthfully.

Every giver must eventually allow themselves to receive. Because when you resist receiving, you rob someone else of the joy of giving. That can't sit well with Givers. You, most of all, know the joy of giving. Of course you want others to have some of that giving feeling for themselves. So, how about a little practice experiencing the joy of receiving, too? For the greater good, if you can't do it for yourself, yet. Otherwise, you keep yourself from ease and flow. You teach others that love is a one-way street. You prevent people from showing you their love for you. Is that the legacy you want to leave?

We told Tom, "Your giving opened something in us. Let us return it and complete the loop." The room shifted.

You could feel it—twelve people who had been held so tenderly for three days now leaning forward, eager to give back. The energy was electric. Eyes bright. Hands reaching. Hearts wide open. We weren't just offering support—we were hungry for it. This was our turn. Our chance to say, "You matter. You're not alone. Let us love you the way you loved us."

And that's what I hope every giver begins to understand.

Permissions You Need to Hear

I want to start by saying something I don't think you hear enough: I love how generous you are. Truly. I admire the way you show up for others, the way you give your time, energy, and heart. Your intentions are absolutely beautiful.

Are you starting to see all the opportunities to be generous that you're missing? They look like letting go. Like saying yes when someone offers to help. Like asking for what you need. Like allowing someone to hold your story, grief, or exhaustion without apology or explanation.

I get it. It feels upside down. But gently, for those who need to hear it again plainly—you are not the only one with something to give. Letting people serve you doesn't make you weak; it makes you wise. It creates space for the people who you love to love you back. It lets them experience the same joy you feel when you give. And when you let them, you are allowing them to become more like you.

You are multiplying your generosity instead of diminishing it.

Here is what I want you to hear today. These are your permissions when you need them. Write them down, tape them to your mirror, or whisper them to yourself when the guilt creeps in:

- You are allowed to rest.
- You are allowed to receive.
- You are allowed to need help.
- You are allowed to ask for what you need instead of only offering what you have.
- You are allowed to let someone else take the lead.
- You are allowed to be loved in return.

You are still generous when you are not giving. You don't disappear when you stop doing. You don't lose your value when you need a minute to breathe. The world won't fall apart if you let someone else take over for a while. In fact, you may be surprised by how beautiful it feels.

So, maybe your most generous act today will be what you allow someone else to do for you. That's putting Infinite Generosity to work.

Growing Your Faith in the Giving State

In the Giving state of Infinite Generosity, faith is about trusting that you're already enough, even when you are not pouring yourself out.

Rose always says that when she dies, she's got questions for God. Who doesn't, right?

She's been through so much. She'll say, "What the heck, man?" But even in the same breath, she'll tell you that every hard thing she's faced has helped to shape her into who she is. Faith lives in the tension between *Why did this happen?* and *I'm so grateful for my life.*

The kind of faith we need as givers is often smaller and quieter than we expect. It's not just faith in a plan or a bigger purpose, though that helps. It's faith that the energy you're putting out into the world will return to you. That your giving is not unnoticed. That the God who sees in secret also sees you. And that you are held even when you're tired and not able to hold it all together alone.

Let me say this again: Your value is not in your giving. It's in who you are. And who you are is already defined by God. Not your calendar, your performance, or your productivity.

I had to learn that the hard way after the accident at my swim school.

For a while, I thought maybe I had lost everything that made me lovable, everything that made me worthy of love. That without my business, my reputation, my role as the capable one—I was nothing.

But what I came to see, slowly and painfully, was that nothing outside of me defines me. Not what I've built. Not what I've lost. Not what people say about me, true or false.

My identity is rooted in God alone. I am who God says I am.

That's it. That's the whole thing.

And for many of us who live in the Giving state, that's the faith we need to grow: the faith that who we are isn't measured by how much we give.

Letting others serve us isn't just rest; it's a spiritual discipline. It's an act of humility. When Jesus washed His disciples' feet, it was an act of generosity and a call to community. To take turns. To serve and be served. To bend low in love, yes, but also to allow others to do the same for us.

That's what we miss when we resist receiving. We miss the chance to grow our faith in humility. To believe, not just in God, but in others. To believe that the infinity loop of generosity will bring us back around. And that the love we give will find its way home to us through someone else's hands.

That takes humility. And I think humility might be the true spiritual practice of the Giving state. Not the kind that says, "I'm worthless," but the kind that says, "I don't have to be everything for everyone. I can trust the goodness in others. I can trust that God defines me."

So, if you find yourself here—loving to give, longing to serve, and lit up by the chance to help—thank God for that. But also ask yourself, "Where is God inviting me to receive? Where might He be asking me to stretch my faith by trusting more instead of doing more?

Growth lives in the quiet faith that lets you receive generosity back.

What's the Generous Thing to Choose Here?

If you're in the Giving state, it can feel like the generous thing to choose is to give more. That's the instinct: to jump in, show up, and act.

But let me offer a deeper question. Instead of asking, "How can I be generous in this situation?", what if you asked, "What is the generous thing to choose here, universally?"

That question invites a broader perspective, doesn't it? It might actually mean allowing yourself to receive, say no, or just be still. The generous thing might be to stop the self-talk that says you're only valuable when you're productive. It might be choosing rest instead of guilt, or taking a breath before you respond.

If you're someone whose identity is built on being a helper, it's easy to assume that generosity always looks like action. But true generosity begins with discernment. Is your giving aligned with joy, intention, and integrity?

Among high-achieving givers, burnout often sneaks in under the guise of commitment. Leaders, business owners, and caretakers give and give, feeling guilty for taking a break. They feel responsible for everyone and everything. But what if the generous thing isn't doing more? What if it's allowing others to step up, too? What if it's receiving the support that's already available?

Sometimes, the generous thing is a pause, a shift, or a choice not to rush. A decision to stay curious long enough to see all the options on the table, not just one that your habits want to choose.

That simple question—what's the generous thing to choose here?—creates possibility. It opens space and invites you to notice when you're giving from overflow and when you're giving from obligation. It lets you check whether your actions are creating a connection or leading you toward resentment.

Because generous living means doing the right thing for you at the right moment, with the right heart. It could be giving, receiving, or doing nothing at all. And sometimes, the most generous thing you can do is to remind yourself, *I've done enough for now.* That's still generosity.

Questions to Ask Yourself

1. When I give, am I offering from a place of joy and overflow, or habit and expectation?
2. What stories have I inherited about what it means to be a "good" giver, and are they still serving me?
3. Where in my life have I mistaken depletion for devotion?
4. What would it look like to give *with* love, not *for* love?
5. If I paused before giving, what other generous options might reveal themselves, toward others or myself?
6. How are my values limiting my definition of generosity?

CHAPTER FOUR

Receiving

Even after discovering that generosity is more than just giving, I still have opportunities that show me how hard it is for me to receive. During a recent sacred plant ceremony, I came to a humbling revelation: I was still operating as if help was something other people deserved, but not me.

The first night was rough, physically and emotionally. My body reacted strongly, and I felt sick for hours. And although I was surrounded by trained facilitators and gentle souls whose job was to support me, and I was asked if I wanted support, I didn't ask for help. The truth is, I didn't know what that meant, "support." Encouraged to be curious about my feelings of sickness, nausea, disgust,

I told myself I was fine. That I could and should handle it alone. I went through that entire experience in the fetal position, observing the feeling of nausea, quietly bracing myself, convinced that holding it alone was somehow more dignified or brave. It didn't occur to me to ask for help.

But on the second night, something shifted.

When I walked up to receive the medicine again, the facilitator, Suzie, looked me in the eyes and said, "I hope you have a wonderful journey. I want you to know that you can ask for help if you need it. But I get the feeling you won't."

There it was. A simple truth laid bare. She didn't say it with judgment, just quiet, clear insight. Like she could see the whole story playing out just beneath the surface. It was a story I'd written for years. The one that equated strength with self-reliance, and self-reliance with silence.

In that moment, I couldn't help but see myself through her eyes. I saw the tension I carried, the invisible pressure to keep it together. And I realized how often I moved through the world like that—not just in a ceremony, but in life. Brushing off offers of help. Sidestepping support. Keeping the spotlight on what I could give while ignoring the ache inside me.

It was a mirror that I didn't ask for. And because I'm not one to be told I can't do something, it was exactly what I needed. *Challenge accepted!*

Because the truth is, we don't become more generous by giving more. We become more generous when we let generosity flow *to* us, not just *from* us. The question isn't just, "How can I give?" It's also, "Where am I still refusing to receive?"

Receiving in those moments isn't weak. It's not lazy, indulgent, or selfish. It's a form of trust. It's letting someone else show up and letting love land.

That night, I started to practice. Slowly and imperfectly. I asked for help when I felt the feeling of disgust return. I knew that my path to peace, healing, and wholeness was in surrendering to my feelings and allowing them to be truly felt and honored. I asked for help and was encouraged and supported in that endeavor. When I thought I might throw up, symbolically eliminating all the emotions of this deep grief, loss, shame, humiliation, anger, blame, sadness, and disgust, Suzie and Tom were there, supporting me with their physical bodies, encouraging my emotional elimination, nodding encouragement and asking gentle questions to bring me along in my journey. This was coupled with a room full of twelve others whose love and support I felt and received as they continued with their individual journeys.

I wanted to forgive. To ultimately stop selecting suffering. I ended up, on ceremony night one, mothering myself and my family. Really feeling that motherly "poor baby" empathy from and for myself and for my family's sufferings after I experienced all the sickness. And that, of course, led me to his family, the Foundation, and all that we had suffered, and that we could continue to suffer. I wanted to break the chain. I wanted off the rollercoaster.

And so I said yes to the offer of support. And it got me here.

And maybe that's where the Receiving state of being begins. Not with a grand act of surrender, but with a quiet, courageous yes.

Yes, I need help. Yes, I'm open. And yes, I'm worthy of care, too. And it all starts with digging deep to find the faith and trust to take the next step.

When Receiving Becomes a Stereotype

Before I started doing real work around receiving, I thought my only problem was asking for help. Turns out, that was just the surface. Underneath was a whole ecosystem of beliefs, reflexes, and buried emotions that shaped how I responded anytime someone offered me support.

What I've come to see through my journey, professionally and personally, is that most of us carry a distorted version of receiving. Not because we're selfish or broken, but because we've absorbed so many conflicting messages about what it means to need or accept help. Some of us overdo it while others avoid it. And some of us try to game it into a kind of emotional transaction.

These aren't permanent identities. They are states we can fall into when something is out of alignment, when our self-worth gets knotted up with our need. You might recognize one of these stereotypes in yourself or others.

Assistance Avoider. They'd rather walk through a blizzard than ask anyone for a ride. The Assistance Avoider insists they've got it all covered, even when it's painfully obvious that they do not. They hate feeling like a burden, so they'll say yes to help just to avoid an argument, but they are secretly squirming the whole time. To them, receiving feels like admitting defeat.

Reciprocal Recipient. Different from the Scorekeeping Supporter, this person keeps a mental checklist of every favor they have ever received. They are determined to pay it all back, and sometimes get stuck feeling guilty when they can't. Even the simplest act of kindness feels like a debt they need to repay. Their obsession with paying back the favor or gift, evening the scales, makes receiving feel more stressful than joyful.

Habitual Beneficiary. This person is always at the front of the line when help is offered. The Habitual Beneficiary never turns down a helping hand, but it's less about need and more about comfort. They have become so accustomed to receiving that they forget to look for ways to give back. It's not that they don't want to help; they just don't see how they can. They are stuck in a cocoon of others' giving and often don't experience the discomfort that might lead to positive change.

Unmotivated Collector. Why do it yourself when someone else will do it for you? The Unmotivated Collector isn't exactly lazy, but they certainly are not proactive. They are stuck in a cycle of waiting for rescue instead of taking initiative. They want to be more independent but feel overwhelmed by where or how to start.

I don't share these patterns to shame anyone. What matters is noticing the moment we're out of sync, and then gently nudging ourselves back into the flow of true Infinite

Generosity, the kind that honors the gift, the giver, and ourselves.

Understanding Yourself in This State

Just like in the Giving state, we can understand the Receiving state by paying attention to the values that live underneath it. Receiving isn't just about taking in support. It's about what it means to need something, to be vulnerable, and to accept care or gratitude from others. For many people, those experiences bump right up against deeply held values like independence, responsibility, pride, and fairness.

Independence is likely one of your strengths. You pride yourself on being capable, self-sufficient, and low-maintenance. You don't want to be a burden. You like solving problems on your own, and you're really good at it. But when independence becomes rigid, it can turn into isolation. You stop letting people in. You convince yourself that needing help is a sign of weakness instead of humanity. And over time, that mindset doesn't just create distance, it creates burnout.

Responsibility is another value that often shapes the Receiving state. You feel a deep sense of duty to the people in your life. You're the one others rely on. You follow through, and you don't want to let anyone down. But if left unchecked, responsibility can turn into martyrdom. This is when you put everyone else first and tell yourself that's what dependability looks like. But if you're always carrying the weight alone, it becomes unsustainable. And if you never speak your needs out loud, resentment has a funny way of leaking through the cracks.

Then there's pride. You've worked hard to become competent, reliable, and in control. Asking for help can feel like you're relinquishing all of that. You might fear it will make you look weak, or worse, indebted. What if something goes wrong? What if you owe them later? These are real questions. But when pride takes the wheel, it can keep you from experiencing the healing that comes from mutual care. It blocks the intimacy and trust that make life rich.

Fairness and modesty can play a part here, too. You might think, *Other people need help more than I do* or *I've already had my share.* That kind of humility can be noble. But when it leads to unnecessary suffering, it becomes a form of self-denial. And over time, it can reinforce the belief that you're only worthy when you aren't asking for anything.

These values are not bad. In fact, they're often evidence of integrity, experience, and a generous heart. But when they go unexamined, they can become barriers. They can keep you stuck in survival mode. They can block creativity, joy, and connection. They can whisper a lie: you are only valuable when you are strong.

So, how do you know when you're in the Receiving state of being?

You'll notice that asking for help feels uncomfortable, maybe even shameful. You might tell yourself it's easier to just do it all. You may struggle to receive gifts, compliments, or kindness without deflecting or diminishing them. You might be deeply tired but feel guilty resting. You'll feel the tension of being someone who gives a lot but rarely lets others return the favor.

When you're receiving, it's essential to remember this: You don't lose value when you need something. You don't become weak when you let yourself be seen. Every time you allow someone else to support you, you're offering them a chance to be generous. You invite connection and contribute to a flow that strengthens both sides of the infinity loop.

Receiving isn't passive, it's brave. It's generous in its own right. And the moment you stop judging yourself for receiving is the moment you begin to move freely through this state, not as someone who is broken, but as someone who is beautifully human.

Doing My Homework

I remember exactly where I was when I realized how deeply uncomfortable I was with receiving. I was in a virtual coaching session with Coach Mike, and he began it by offering me a genuine acknowledgment. It was one of those slow, thoughtful recognitions that comes from someone really seeing you. He was praising something I had done well. It was a beautifully kind moment.

And then I felt it. Not the compliment or the love from my coach. The shutdown.

My brain just clicked off. Like I reached up and flipped a switch inside myself. He continued, and I smiled and nodded, but I wasn't fully there. I didn't feel much more than static. As soon as he finished, I found myself responding with, "Awesome. Does that mean you're going to give me a discount on my next round of coaching?"

Yeah, that's what I said.

He didn't laugh. He just looked right at me, not with anger but with clarity. His expression said everything: *That's not what I said. That's not what I meant. That's not what this was.*

We wrapped up the call, and I sat there, stunned by my own deflection. I knew what I had done. I had taken a beautifully wrapped gift and chose not to accept it. And he knew it, too.

On our next call, I apologized. To his credit, he didn't dwell on it. Instead, he gave me an assignment. He said, "I want you to start paying attention. Notice what people give you. Kindness, compliments, and acknowledgment. Pay attention to how your body reacts when someone offers you something, especially something you didn't earn or work for."

I'll admit, it felt pretty silly at first. But I did it. And the more I practiced, the more I realized how often I tended to bat generosity away. I could give all day, but receiving? That stirred up something else entirely. Something vulnerable that felt like exposure.

Then, a few months later, my daughter and I went to see Taylor Swift in concert.

We were in a stadium filled with tens of thousands of people. The lights dropped, the crowd roared, and Taylor stepped out onto that stage. Between her opening song and the next one ("The Man," for all you Swifties out there), she just stood there. She didn't rush or shrink. She just took it in.

She turned slowly, section by section, soaking up every ounce of love and energy the people were giving her. It was full-body receiving, without apology or deflection. It wasn't performative or arrogant. It was pure love.

Watching her, I felt something click into place. That's what it can look like. Not greed, ego, or vanity. Just honest gratitude. A deep breath that says, *Thank you. I see it. I feel it. I'm going to take a moment to let it land.*

That night, Taylor Swift became another one of my teachers. And my coach did, too. Because what they both showed me—him, in our awkward, honest moment, and her in that sweeping, shimmering one—was that receiving isn't passive. It's active participation in the present moment. And most of all, it's permission.

We're not meant to muscle through life by giving endlessly while refusing to be filled. Infinite Generosity isn't one-sided and stagnant. It's fluid. And the more I can let it flow, the more complete and connected I feel.

Permissions You Need to Hear

If you are receiving, I want to offer you some gentle truths that may feel strange at first, but are meant to help you restore your sense of wholeness.

Receiving is not a failure of strength, a reflection of your inadequacy, or a sign that you are broken or incapable.

It's just your turn. Plain and simple. And you are allowed to take your turn.

You may be carrying a quiet, even stubborn belief that accepting help makes you weak, selfish, or burdensome. You may have learned to equate being needed with being valuable. So when the roles shift and you find yourself needing support, you feel exposed. Maybe even ashamed. You want to give back right away or disappear altogether.

Hear me when I say you are not weak because you are receiving. And you are not selfish for needing something. Everyone needs help. Everyone struggles. The story that says you should be exempt is a lie dressed up as a virtue.

Some seasons will feel like a desert. You'll look around and feel unsure of what you have to offer. But even deserts bloom. When you're low on energy, hope, or clarity, you can still show up with something beautiful. It might be as simple as telling someone how they helped you, offering a word of encouragement, or just being present and honest with where you are. That's enough.

You are allowed to stop measuring your worth by what you lack. This is where that beautiful idea from *The Gap and the Gain*[1] comes in. When we're stuck in the receiving state and it feels like we're in deficit mode, our brains naturally focus on the gap—the distance between where we are and where we wish we were. And that's a puny place to live. It shrinks us, zaps our creativity, and makes receiving feel shameful and filled with *shoulds*. But what if you measured backwards instead? What if you looked at how far you've come instead of how far you still have to go? That shift from gap to gain is powerful. Because when you see your progress, you feel want instead of need. Want is active and creative. It says, "*I've made it this far. Imagine what's next.*" It reawakens your agency, energy, and generosity.

You have permission to re-enter the flow of Infinite Generosity, even while receiving. Maybe you're not in a position to give back directly to the person who helped you, but you can give forward. That's what I've come to understand. Generosity doesn't have to be reciprocal to be meaningful. When we give without keeping score, we position ourselves to ask, "What are my gifts that I can share right now, as I am?" and we get to reconnect with abundance. We step out of shame and begin to float again.

There's a New Radicals song with the lyric, "You only get what you give."[2] And I used to believe that as a way of life. Givers get. Not because they're expecting a return, but because they're in the flow of movement, momentum, and motion. As a receiver, your opportunity isn't to repay, but to stay in motion. To let the energy of what you've received move through you and out into the world in some new way.

You are not puny or broken. You are simply in a season where the gift is yours to receive. Your receiving might be someone else's gift, healing, or fulfillment of purpose. Letting them show up for you is an act of generosity in itself. Think about that. Your yes gives them the chance to be a giver. And not just any giver, but the right one at the right time.

This state is asking you to be a generous receiver. That means saying yes to support, care, recognition, and kindness without twisting them into proof that something is wrong with you. It means accepting a compliment with a simple "Thank you." It means letting love land without immediately trying to repay it. Or letting yourself be carried when you're tired, so you'll have the strength again later.

Receiving is part of generosity, not the opposite. It's the balance.

And if you keep blocking help because you think it's noble or selfless, I want to lovingly challenge that train of thought. It's not always selfless to say no. It can feel incredibly selfish to the people who love you the most, those who want to be there for you but keep getting waved off.

Don't let pride get in the way of intimacy. Let yourself be loved. Let yourself be helped. Let the goodness in. That's your permission, and that's a step toward wholeness.

Growing Your Faith in the Receiving State

If the Giving state of being is about learning to see yourself the way God sees you, the Receiving state is learning to let yourself be seen by others. This is especially true when you're not producing, performing, or proving anything. That's a radical kind of faith. It asks you to believe that love is not earned through effort, and that receiving is a way of staying in flow with the divine.

Consider the story of Mary and Martha in the Bible. Martha is busy. She's doing everything right by cultural and religious standards as she hosts, serves, and prepares. She is giving. And then there's Mary, sitting at Jesus's feet, listening, not helping or rushing around their home. She's just being. When Martha protests, Jesus doesn't shame Mary. Instead, He offers a correction to Martha by saying, "Mary has chosen what is better, and it will not be taken from her."

That line is striking, isn't it? Not because it pits sisters against each other, but because it reveals how differently we can react to the act of receiving. For Martha, receiving in that moment feels like laziness or irresponsibility. But for Mary, it is sacred. She is fully open, present, and trusting that being in communion with Jesus is enough.

Martha is definitely not going with the flow. She is overextended, emotionally reactive, and likely feeling unseen for all she's doing and feeling a bit abandoned by Mary. Mary, by contrast, is in flow, feeling connected, peaceful, and rooted. And in that moment, Jesus gently reminds us that we were not created to earn love. We were meant to dwell in it.

There's another story that reveals the inner resistance we often feel in the Receiving state: the story of Peter and Jesus at the Last Supper.

Jesus begins to wash His disciples' feet, taking the posture of a servant. When He gets to Peter, he protests, telling Jesus He'll never wash his feet. It's uncomfortable, and it feels backward, like an inversion of roles. But Jesus replies, "Unless I wash you, you will have no part with me."

That's a strong statement. And again, not a rebuke, but an invitation to have a relationship. Jesus isn't just teaching humility. He's offering Peter a glimpse of what real intimacy looks like—the ability to give and receive, to serve and be served, to trust and be trusted.

Peter's initial refusal says everything about the way pride, discomfort, and false humility can block connection. He's struggling to receive because he doesn't yet understand that allowing Jesus to care for him is actually faith and partnership rather than weakness.

When you receive, the invitation is to let others in. To stop performing for your worth and start practicing being present. To let go of managing impressions and start opening your heart. It requires vulnerability, trust, and the courage to let generosity move through you, not just as a giver, but as a beloved child of God who can be seen, supported, and celebrated.

In both of these stories, we see the tension that can arise within this state of being. One is external (*Why aren't you doing more?*), and the other is internal (*I can't let you do this for me*).

Both highlight how faith isn't just about believing in God. It's about believing that you are worth loving, even when you aren't giving anything in return.

To grow your faith in this state, ask yourself:

- Can I let someone else care for me without guilt?
- Can I let God's love land, even when I feel unworthy?

- Can I believe that being loved is not the same as being indebted?

Faith in the Receiving state is a posture of openness. It trusts that generosity isn't a one-way street. It's a circle, a flow, and sometimes, the most faithful thing you can do is sit still, open your hands, and say yes to love.

What's the Generous Thing to Choose Here?

As I write this chapter, I'm still asking myself this question when it comes to receiving. For the majority of my life, I've believed that generosity only flows in one direction, from giver to receiver. But I'm learning that there are moments when the most generous act isn't offering help, it's accepting it.

Recently, I was celebrating a milestone: my five hundredth session as an EOS Implementer. One of the teams I work with wanted to commemorate the achievement with a gift— a personalized Yeti cooler, complete with a special engraving. It was thoughtful, meaningful, and honestly, a little uncomfortable.

Why? I didn't need that. And the idea of picking out my own gift (or worse, rejecting theirs) made me feel awkward and self-conscious. Like I was choreographing my own celebration.

That's the tension we face in this state. When we're used to being the giver, it's hard to switch roles. To let someone else plan, offer, provide, or honor us, we start negotiating with ourselves: "Is this necessary? Is it wasteful? Am I being too much?" But beneath those thoughts is often something deeper: a resistance to being seen.

Because receiving, at its core, is about allowing yourself to be recognized. Not for what you've done, but for who you are and what you mean to someone else.

This brings us back to the question: "What's the generous thing to choose here?"

Not "What's the polite thing to do?" or "What would make me most comfortable?" but "What would honor the moment and the people who want to mark it with me?"

The generous thing, I realized, was just to receive. Not necessarily the Yeti cooler, but the intention behind it. The effort, love, and appreciation.

Rejecting the gift might seem humble, but if I'm honest, it would have sent the opposite message. It would have batted their love out of the air. It would have protected my pride at the cost of their joy.

So I softened. I let it in. Not because I needed the object, but because I understood the connection. Sometimes the most generous thing we can do is say, "Thank you"—and really mean it.

Let the compliment rest in your heart, let the offer stand, and let the celebration unfold, even if it makes you squirm a little.

Generosity isn't always about doing something. Sometimes it's about not blocking what others want to do for you. It's about receiving without shrinking, deflecting, or turning it into a transaction.

So if you're in a moment like this and feel uncertain about how to respond to the gift, offer, or acknowledgment, pause and ask yourself, "What's the generous thing to choose here?" Then follow your heart. Especially if it's uncomfortable. That discomfort is a sign that you're growing, stretching, and practicing a fuller kind of generosity: the kind that flows.

Questions to Ask Yourself

1. What do I believe it says about me if I need help?
2. Do I offer support freely but resist receiving it? If so, why?
3. What has made receiving feel safe and comfortable in the past?
4. What are the worst and best things that could happen if I receive?
5. How can I become a generous receiver?

CHAPTER FIVE

Observing

The day I went to Home Depot for some heat guns is seared into my memory. I needed them to help me peel the Love to Swim School vinyl wrap off my car.

That might sound like a straightforward errand, but the truth is, it was one of the most emotionally complex things I've had to do in my life. I was weary from being seen, but all the pulling and peeling felt like I was erasing a part of my identity. It felt like hiding. Not just hiding, disappearing.

I loved that wrap. It was colorful and vibrant, featuring pictures of our young students, including an infant swimming, a baby who loved the water with confidence and skill. It said "from *Won't* to *Watch Me*" on one side, and "from *Can't* to *Confident*" on the other—that's the part I loved the most—progress, possibility. This business was my baby, certainly something I conceived and birthed. And then I nurtured and grew it, with the intention of making a difference in the community. So many beautiful people contributed to this dream of mine. I was feeling shame and humiliation. I was absolutely embarrassed and disgusted. I was so profoundly disappointed in us: the school event staff, the leadership, the public, the people on the deck who failed in their duty, myself.

The day I took the wrap off, I felt a strange moment of relief. Like I was taking a step toward emotional safety. Like I was no longer a moving billboard for a grief I couldn't control. But the next morning, I woke up feeling run over. My body felt heavy, weighed down. It was hard to move. Every day, when I woke up and remembered his death, I found that I would have to re-accept reality. On this morning, once I got to acceptance, I realized that I didn't just remove a logo the night before. Mentally and emotionally, I lost a legacy, a life's work, and a confidence in my identity. That car had been a symbol of who I was for years. It showed the world what I built, what I stood for, and what I gave my life to. And just like that, it was gone.

I had some time to revisit this memory with Rose recently. She listened, the way only Rose can when your heart is aching and you don't have the words. It wasn't just the car. It was everything the car represented. Back then, I felt like I had to disappear, not out of guilt or shame, but out of survival. I needed a break from being seen. Because being seen meant being misunderstood.

There was a time in the years following Mitchell's death when I was actually positioned as a predator—someone who lured families into an unsafe place for profit. There were others saying I was criminally responsible for the death of a child. I have to pause here in case you missed it. *Criminally* responsible.

Try that on.

Lies were published on public platforms, and letters were written to demand that I not be allowed to work with children or that I not be allowed to speak or tell the story from my perspective. There was a cease-and-desist letter sent when my husband got lumped into the blame and misinformation. Stories were being made up about me. About us. Some I never heard, and others I wish I could forget.

Having your face and name associated with the worst moment of someone else's life does something to your nervous system. It's not just sad or painful. It's traumatic. And trauma often leads us into the Observing state, whether we realize it or not.

For me, the Observing state didn't start as a spiritual practice. It started as a survival strategy. I wanted to hide, shrink, and become invisible. Not because I had done something wrong, but because the grief, the blame, and the public scrutiny were all just too much.

So, I retreated.

Here's what I want you to understand: The retreat wasn't all darkness. There was light, too. There still is. In the absence of constant action, I got quiet enough to hear my thoughts. I had long, honest conversations with God about who I was, truly, and who He made me to be. My head was bowed before Him. *Show me Your way, Your will, Your path. Please share Your wisdom. I haven't got the answers. I know that. What would You have me know, Lord?* I learned to ask.

And then I learned—am learning—to listen for the answers. Let myself be guided. Let myself be led. That's the paradox of this state of being. Sometimes we enter the Observing state out of fear, and other times we enter it out of reverence, for the self, for the soul, and for our own need to breathe again. The practice is anchoring in the truth of who we are and who we intend to be.

That day with the heat gun was both dark and light. A moment of running and a moment of release. A retreat and a reckoning. And a quiet choice to disappear just long enough to try and find myself again. The Observing state can hold both sides at once: avoidance and truth, distance and discernment, silence and a sacred space where the next version of you is slowly, quietly being shaped.

When Observing Becomes a Stereotype

The Observing state can be a sacred and essential pause. It allows us to step back, reflect, process, and protect what matters most. But when we stay too long in this space, or enter it for reasons we are not fully aware of, it can morph into something more rigid. We start retreating not just for rest, but for control. We guard ourselves not just for wisdom, but out of fear.

Sometimes our withdrawal is a form of self-respect. Other times, it's a quiet cry for safety. And often, we don't realize we're stuck in the Observing state until someone gently asks us, "Where did you go?"

To help name the patterns we might encounter in this state, here are a few familiar characters who can show up when the world feels too loud, too fast, too cruel, or too uncertain.

The Lone Wolf. This person retreats from the world and finds himself or herself in a curated bubble instead of a cave. They might still attend meetings or show up for dinner, but emotionally, they have unplugged. They crave solitude, stillness, and long walks without anyone asking how they're doing. It isn't that they don't care; it's that caring too much, too often, has left them depleted. They are recharging, but also quietly hoping the world doesn't come knocking until they are ready.

The Relocationist. Life gets hard, and this person moves, literally or metaphorically. They change houses, cities, jobs, or belief systems. Reinvention is their survival strategy. When things feel unsafe or untrustworthy, they respond with a dramatic shift in scenery, hoping it will bring emotional safety with it. They are not afraid to start over, but their constant evolution can sometimes be a disguise for fear of being known or staying still long enough to feel the weight of their situation.

The Safety Skeptic. This person used to trust easily. Now, everyone is on trial. Period, the end. They read between the lines of every single text message, second-guess the motives behind every compliment, and wait for the catch. Their favorite word is discernment, and while it has saved them more than once, it has become their armor. They're not unkind. They're just unwilling to be fooled again. Vulnerability is something they give out in teaspoons, and only after repeated evidence that it's safe to do so.

The Growth-Addicted Seeker. Learning their way through healing is the modus operandi of this person. They don't isolate in silence. They isolate in podcasts, retreats, courses, and books. On the surface, they seem active and engaged, but they are mostly participating in controlled environments where vulnerability is timed and structured. They may begin growing, but they are also using growth as a buffer between themselves and actual connection. Their constant question is, "What am I supposed to learn from this?" Sometimes, what they really need is to feel and not fix.

If you saw a glimpse of yourself in any of these types, you are not alone. We build walls when we're in pain, pause to gather strength, and retreat when we're overwhelmed. None of that is wrong.

But the longer we stay in hiding, the harder it becomes to know what we're protecting and why. At some point, we stop observing and start avoiding. That's where our growth gets stuck.

The gift of the Observing state of being isn't isolation; it's insight. And insight brings us back into the flow of Infinite Generosity when we share it. So when you feel ready, let yourself be seen again, and let what you've learned help you start to move.

Understanding Yourself in This State

There's a particular stillness that can settle over you when you're in the Observing state of being. It's not quite rest, and it's not always a retreat to some new scenery or break from your day-to-day. It's something quieter, more inward. You aren't disengaged from life, but you aren't diving into the middle of it either. You're watching from the edge, gathering information, protecting what's tender, and deciding what's safe to share and what still needs time.

For me, it's where I go when the world gets too loud or too cruel. It's where I find my footing again. But it hasn't always been easy to stay there without slipping into fear or isolation. Because while the Observing state holds wisdom and discernment, it also holds pain.

Often, we enter this state because something hurts. Maybe someone betrayed our trust, or something overwhelmed our nervous system. And our values are trying to protect us. Values like privacy, discernment, emotional safety, and control. They are beautiful and essential. But like all powerful things, they can cut both ways.

Privacy can feel like peace, especially when the outside world has misused your vulnerability. For years, I confused secrecy with privacy. My mind was continually putting me on trial, reviewing evidence at every turn, as many of us do in grief and sorrow. I thought that to live in integrity and own what is mine in this tragedy I had to tell everyone everything, right up front, in an attempt to beat them to the punch. "Here it is," I imagined myself saying, "the story you think you already know." I wore it like a scarlet letter. I even tried this identity: *I am responsible for the death of a child.* I let that sentence echo in my heart for a while. I tested it to see if it was true. I asked myself, again and again, *What am I accountable for? What do I own?* And *how can I ever make it right?*

During this state, I needed to sit with those questions and all the emotions attached to the answers I gave myself, in silence, reflection, and prayer. When public condemnation and lies were launched against me personally, I stayed in this state even longer. My silence wasn't weakness. It felt like protection, grief, and discernment. It also weirdly felt like generosity, too. It was like the most generous thing I could do was be quiet, take no risks, and therefore do no harm.

That's one of the beautiful aspects of being in the Observing state: We learn to listen, pause, and seek the truth beyond the outside noise. We take the time for careful, thoughtful choices rather than reactive ones. We have the space to evaluate motives and protect our peace as we seek clarity and the truth of who we are—who God has created us to be.

I was getting right with myself.

No. I was not responsible for the death of a child.

No. I am not responsible.

I am accountable for it. It was my business. And I can say with absolute confidence that the training, experience, protocol, and credentials were all there.

If we follow the impulse to stay in the Observing state indefinitely, we can slide into mistrust or withdrawal. When we protect ourselves too much, we can become inaccessible, not just to others, but to ourselves. We begin to believe that being unseen is safer than being misunderstood. We build walls and consider ourselves wise for doing so. But if we keep building them, it's easy to fall into isolation. It's also easy to get stuck playing small, shrinking your gifts and talents, holding back what you have to offer out of fear and exhaustion.

I've learned that we can move through the positive and negative sides of this state, sometimes within the same hour. There are days when I am brave enough to feel everything: the disgust, grief, shame, and fury. I honor it all. In doing so, I honor the people I love. That moment on the medicine journey in Denver, when I felt the full weight of it all from all sides and everyone involved, was absolutely sacred. It wasn't an inward collapse. It was honoring. And in that honoring, something inside me was released. Not erased, but softened and witnessed.

The Observing state of being offers us the chance to bear witness to the hidden truth of our own experiences, and to the quiet strength it takes to evaluate them objectively. What if you gave yourself the grace and mercy you give to everyone else? We pause, notice, and discern. And when the moment is right, we choose how to move forward with love.

This is not a state to rush. It's one to respect. If this is where you find yourself, ask, "Am I hiding, or am I healing? Am I frozen, or am I finding my faith again?" The answers matter. And the fact that you're asking means you're already beginning to understand yourself in this state.

Get Out of the Boat

When I stepped into the EOS community full of entrepreneurs and Implementers, I didn't feel brave. I felt exposed.[3]

Grateful for a new opportunity? Yes.

Curious and ready to learn? Yes.

But underneath it all, I was still carrying the weight of who I used to be. I didn't know how to be anyone else yet. I was rebuilding my life, but I was still dragging around the heavy winter coat of grief I couldn't take off. I carried guilt, sadness, failure, and loss with me. The invisible burden of a reputation that no longer matched my integrity. The internal ache of being defined by a horrific tragedy still had a way of ebbing and flowing throughout my days.

When I showed up at my first EOS Quarterly Collaborative Exchange (QCE), the day after Implementer boot camp, I was still trying to remember who I was and deciding whether I belonged. I knew, as an entrepreneur, that I had experience to share, but I wasn't confident about how I could contribute meaningfully. And that was my consistent prayer: *Please help me find a way to use the gifts, skills, and talents I've been given to contribute meaningfully.* I was conflicted about this new path. And also resigned to it. *I can recreate myself,* I thought. I had spent most of my adult life clear about my contribution to drowning prevention and water safety. To doing good work in the community by providing a service and jobs that developed people and families, making them better. Now, in observing everyone else, I felt unsure if I had anything to offer.

But the EOS community, like the U.S. Swim School Association before it, met me with something unexpected: grace, encouragement, generosity, and curiosity. No one asked me to prove my worth. They just made space for me to find it again.

That's what connection looks like when you are in the Observing state. You are not reaching out with both arms yet. You show up quietly. You listen, learn, and watch. And when the time is right, you will move.

There was one moment I'll never forget. It was in that first QCE, when I was still wrestling with the identity crisis I hadn't yet named out loud. I met Derrick Smith, a principal team member of the Firefly Group, the private equity owners of EOS Worldwide. More than that, he was part of an Implementer prayer group I'd joined.

When he first heard my story, he was heartbroken for all of us, as most are. Though our initial meeting was brief, he kept me in his prayers, he reached out to me periodically, and reminded me that we would inevitably catch up at QCE. Over time, I shared how painful this tragedy was and how fueled I felt to make his death matter. "What did God want me to do with this tragedy?" was a consistent question. I shared some of my story with him. Just the raw outlines. The weight I was carrying, the hope I didn't know how to claim, and the fear that maybe I'd always carry around this heavy coat of catastrophic loss. I was so tired. The kind of tired no amount of sleep can cure.

He looked at me and said, "Remember Peter. Don't stay in the boat when God is calling you out."

When he said it, I didn't really understand what he meant. I only knew that what he was saying was important. I had to look it up and study it. It became a pebble in my shoe. I even printed a picture with those words on it that I keep in my office. His advice that day put to words what I was afraid to admit: I was still in the boat. Watching the waves while others walked, waiting for permission to move. Lacking the faith that God will provide a way, if we listen, hear, and heed Him.

The Observing state can keep you safe. It can give you time to heal. But if you're not careful, it can also become a hiding place, a holding pattern, or a spiritual freeze.

Derrick's words reminded me that Observing isn't the end of the journey. It's the pause before the next one. It's the moment you take stock, then take a step. And sometimes, that step looks like signing up for a new kind of bootcamp, starting a new business, or learning something completely outside of your comfort zone. For me, it was learning to trust my gifts in a room where people didn't know my past.

It wasn't easy. I still felt shaky, but each time I sat across from a business owner or their leadership team, as they listened with care and helped us find clarity, I felt something in me coming back to life. I was still observing, but I was no longer retreating. I was choosing, moving, and believing that I was called to—and still could—contribute meaningfully in this world.

That's the connection I found in this state, not just with others, but with God. Because faith doesn't always look like standing tall; sometimes, it looks like getting out of the boat while your legs still feel weak. Other times, it looks like sitting in a room full of strangers, only to realize they are your new people. It can even look like letting go of what you were known for so you can become who you were made to be.

Permissions You Need to Hear

If you find yourself in the Observing state, I want to encourage you by saying it makes sense for you to be here. Whatever led you here—trauma, betrayal, burnout, loss, or just the need to breathe—you are in the right place.

This is the state where you step back, get quiet, stop overfunctioning, and start listening to your own soul again. There is a difference between hiding and healing, and it's okay if you don't always know which one you are doing.

You might need to isolate to feel safe or disappear from the noise of your own thoughts. One of my mentors, George Block, reminded me of something that changed everything:

I don't have to engage in or respond to every comment or question. Not every accusation deserves a defense. Not every misunderstanding requires correction. Not every invitation needs an RSVP.

At first, that felt impossible. My instinct was to respond, to clarify, to set the record straight. But George helped me see that engaging with every attack, every distortion, every demand for explanation was keeping me trapped in other people's narratives. It was giving away my power—handing it over to anyone who wanted to pull me back into the fray.

When I finally gave myself permission to be silent, to not participate in the ongoing trial of my character, something shifted. I stopped bleeding energy into battles I didn't need to fight. I reclaimed my attention, my peace, my sense of self. That advice helped me regain some of my power—not by fighting harder, but by choosing not to fight at all.

Remember, retreating isn't weakness, it's wisdom.

You *are* allowed to take a break. You don't owe the world your constant participation. You *are not* selfish for needing rest or silence. Stepping away *isn't* failing. You are honoring your limits, and that is a form of strength.

You *don't have to* say yes to everyone. Boundaries don't need to be explained, and you don't have to justify your hesitation. Discernment is a gift that helps you choose what is healthy, safe, and true in the moment for you. If you've been hurt, being slow to re-engage is a wise choice every time.

The Observing state often invites a flood of feelings, like grief, anger, anxiety, and confusion. Maybe it's all bubbling up now because you are finally giving yourself the space to feel them. Congratulations and well done for allowing those feelings to be felt. That makes you honest, not weak. You do not have to fix it all today. Just be present with it, in your body and your soul, and let it teach you something true about yourself. Listen to it. Be open. A question I have adopted from the work of Elizabeth Gilbert is to ask God, the Universe, Spirit (GUS for short) the simple question, "What would you have me know?"[4]

There is a sacredness to privacy, to tending to your interior life without the distraction and evaluation of performance or proof; learning not to wear your "failures" or mistakes like a scarlet letter; learning to take yourself down from the stand of your ongoing trial, to stop and evaluate the truth of all the judgement and prosecution. The quest here, if there is one, is to be a truth seeker. *What's really true? Is that really true?* Those are good questions to filter thoughts and opinions through. You are not being secretive here. You are being honored and, to some degree, holy. This is your space to restore your inner world, reconnecting with the divine in you, before re-entering the outer one.

Some days, the Observing state feels like a sabbatical, and other days, it can feel like exile. There will be days when you wake up grounded and go to bed spiraling. That's okay. This state is fluid. You are allowed to move in and out of the shadows without judgment. You are not trapped here; you're just in process.

You are allowed to hope again. I know it's scary. It can hurt to want things again and to imagine that maybe things could be good. Hope is part of healing. And you're allowed to have it, even if it comes in fragile waves that barely tap at your toes before flowing away again.

In this state, you are not broken or behind. You are in the sacred, quiet middle of something. It's okay to let that be enough for now. Because this state is not the end of your generosity, it's the pause that protects it.

Growing Your Faith in the Observing State

When everything in us feels guarded and searching, we can keep returning to the story in Matthew 14, where the disciples are in a boat, in the middle of a storm, and Jesus comes walking toward them on the water.

At first, they are terrified. They don't recognize Him. And then He says the words we all need to hear in the middle of chaos: "Take courage. It is I. Don't be afraid."

What comes next is the part that I find useful to remember. Peter is still unsure, and he says, "Lord, if it's really you, tell me to come to you on the water."

And Jesus says, "Come."

That's it. No instructions on how to stay on top of the water. No safety net. Just one word. Come.

It's a moment of observation, followed by faith. Peter is assessing, discerning, and testing what is true in his head. But then he moves. He steps out of the boat.

That is what faith in the Observing state looks like.

You've been sitting in your own boat, watching, listening, and assessing what feels safe and what doesn't. You've needed that time. And if you've ever tried to trust again after pain, you know what this feels like. You are not going to go bounding out of the boat. It's slow, and maybe even methodical, but you're moving forward.

This state of being is often misunderstood as detachment or withdrawal. But I'm learning to see it as a space where discernment and faith meet. We ask the question and wait for the answer before moving. There is a surrendering in that.

Faith in the Observing state is knowing that sometimes stepping out is risky, but staying hidden can cost you even more. You don't have to have it all figured out. You just have to listen, look for the invitation, and take one brave step.

What's the Generous Thing to Choose Here?

Sometimes, when I'm in the Observing state, the most generous thing I can do is absolutely nothing. I mean it. Not in a cold or disengaged way, but in a grounded, self-honoring way. Because presence is powerful when it's real.

There have been days when I didn't have the energy to explain myself. When engaging would have cost more than I had to give, and silence was discernment. In those moments, the generous thing to do was to trust that stepping back was a decision to preserve my integrity instead of pretending I was okay.

Then there are days when I sense someone reaching toward me, hoping I'll let them in. And the generous thing to do is to let them sit beside me in the quiet, letting them know I see them. I'm still here, regrouping.

And they are teaching me who I could be for others in this state, if I choose.

Generosity in the Observing state is learning to make peace with the paradox: one moment, the most generous offering is your honest absence, and the next, it's your quiet return.

Questions to Ask Yourself

1. What am I protecting, and what might I be missing by staying hidden?
2. Is this pause giving me life, or is it starting to cost me connections?
3. Am I trusting my discernment, or am I stuck in a space of overthinking?
4. Who could I let in, even just a little more?
5. What would it look like to honor myself today?
6. Taylor Swift says your energy is a luxury item. Where are you wasting your precious energy right now?

CHAPTER SIX

Floating

There are moments when life asks something from you that your ego cannot answer. You're standing in a room, heart pounding and breath shallow, and everything in your body wants to protect itself, fight back, shut down, prove your worth, or disappear. But something softer and wiser from your heart steps forward instead. That's floating.

It was four years after Mitchell died. I had been invited back to speak at the U.S. Swim School Association spring conference, the very same event I was attending the night I received the call that he had drowned. I had spoken at that first event, back when everything was before the accident. And now, years later, I was returning not just as a member or a former swim school business owner, but as someone who was living the very nightmare we were all working so hard to prevent.

I didn't want to just tell a sad story, though I felt deep sorrow, or position myself as an expert, as if I knew something they didn't, or as a lecturer, though I was continually searching for the lessons. That all felt performative, and it wasn't honest to the experience. I kept asking myself, *How can I make this meaningful? What do I want them to know, feel, see, and act upon?*

Rose and I came up with a format that felt more like us. She would interview me live. That way, it wasn't a monologue. It was a conversation—something held and shared. I spent years thinking about what happened, how it happened, and what could have or should have been done to prevent it. Rose and I, through our regular Saturday calls, wrestled with what my colleagues needed to know about what happened, and what I needed to say to somehow make this awfulness matter.

But about a week before it was time to speak, I was handed a letter from the Foundation that continued to vilify me. The letter was addressed to the president of the U.S. Swim School Association, Tracy Koleber. It was a list of all of my perceived failures, point by point. An indictment that accused me of being reckless, careless, greedy, and dishonest, again. Nine bullet-pointed lines filled with crushing, pain-filled blame. They wanted it read aloud to the full membership so that the membership—my colleagues and friends, who I had served with as a board member and as the vice president and president elect—could understand what a liar and failure I was.

Tracy made her own choice. With compassion, clarity, and insight, she called me to say, "This is yours. You get to decide what to do with it." She then emailed the letter to me.

She was able to separate the emotion and motivation of a grieving mother, while at the same time recognizing the letter's hyperbole and senseless, misinformed accusations. I had stayed quiet for four years, fearing that speaking would do more harm to this grieving family. And, by doing that, I realize now, I lost my voice and, in a very real way, my power, and the Foundation lost access to a truer, more gracious narrative. I didn't stand up for myself or for all the magical people who helped create and perpetuate Love to Swim School for over twenty years. Thankfully, the Association didn't just view me as a subject of a controversial letter, but as a fellow member of the organization. Tracy's kindness, her empathy, and shared business experience gave me back my agency, my first effort at making meaning of this terrible tragedy. And I made my own decision.

I wasn't going to pretend it didn't exist. I wasn't going to bury it in bitterness and anger. I was going to meet it in love.

Those words make it sound so simple. It sure wasn't that simple. It cost me something.

But I asked myself in that moment the question I keep bringing to you: *What's the generous thing to choose here? I mean, really, who am I going to be? And implicit in the question of what the generous thing is to choose here is another even deeper, most important question: How can I love her? What could show her my heart while I did my best to be cognizant of hers?*

So, during the live interview with Rose, she helped me bring it into the open. "I understand the Foundation sent a letter of objection to this talk to Tracy, our president," she said. "What did you decide to do with it?"

And I read it. All of it. I read the accusations aloud and responded to each point one by one. Sometimes I said, "Yes, she is right about this." Like when it said the staff failed to adhere to our 1:8 swimmer/coach ratio because the guard left the pool deck against protocol and training. Other times, I clarified where I disagreed, like when it said I failed to provide staff with lifeguard and drowning recognition training. I owned what was mine, I rejected what wasn't, and I reminded the room that it wasn't a story about one person's failure. No one on that shift went to work that day with the intention to hurt anyone. And, it was an entirely preventable accident. The responsibility for his death is shared. And now, it could be transformed.

That moment became a ripple. This accident impacted if and how swim schools offer recreational swim. It reminded everyone that there is no such thing as common sense, that what is most important, job one no matter what, is to keep people safe. Asking the question: "What is the most important thing you are here to do?" at the beginning of every shift was one way to refocus priorities. It was an important insight after learning more about what happened and what didn't. Based on the staff experience, training, and credentials, what we learned is that even (and especially) your most experienced people can lose sight of what's most important. Complacency is a creeper. You can't assume that someone understands the critical nature of their vigilance in a front-of-mind way; you have to put it there relentlessly. Again and again. And it wasn't just my ripple.

Because what was really happening underneath that exchange was generosity. Tracy's choice was to let me decide what to do with the letter. Rose's presence beside me. My openness and the room's willingness to listen without rushing to judgment. Even the Foundation's letter, though it was painful, became a tool to uncover clarity for all of us. It invited me into a deeper wisdom, a clear path for choosing love. And all of this unfolded within my Learn to Swim business community, in my entrepreneurial circle, in a space that had also held me and supported me in love. That balance mattered. The letter wasn't the whole story. The generosity around it helped carry the weight.

Looking back at that moment caused me to pause as I revisited the memory. It was extremely vulnerable, so exposing. But it also revealed something true. If we ultimately get to the heart of Infinite Generosity, it's love. God's love. And love doesn't always show up in soft, fluffy tones and cozy comfort. Sometimes love is firm, it's challenging made-up stories, it's clarity about what's most important, and it's telling the truth when it would be easier to disappear.

That moment is what floating is all about. It isn't passivity or detachment. It's asking, *Are you here, in it? Or are you watching yourself from above it?* And sometimes the answer is yes. Sometimes, you are lost in the flow and don't realize it until you come back to your breath, like meditation. You only notice you've wandered when you wake back up to stillness.

That's why the pause matters. When we can slow down enough, when we can create space for possibility, we can choose how to respond. Instead of reacting from pride, fear, shame, or anger, we can drop into our hearts and look for a loving, generous response. This is soul work. I don't always find this easy. Sometimes it is breathless and roiling. But for me, the only way I know how to do this soul work is to follow The One who taught me how.

I was blessed. I had found my way back to my Catholic faith and, with it, an example. A leader. So many times, as I learned to walk this path in the after, I looked back at Jesus and asked, What *did* Jesus do? I saw His own humiliation. His own shame and doubts. His own unwavering resolution to love and be loved, no matter the cost. Jesus became my Trusted Guide, my Light, and my Path.

In that moment, I had to ask myself: *Who are you going to be?* Walk your own talk. Walk the same mercy you are begging for. Embody the love you claim to believe in. That was the choice. And it's a choice we all get to make every single day.

Understanding Yourself in This State

Floating isn't a state of being that we can master as it pertains to Infinite Generosity. It's a state we can return to rather than a permanent address or badge we earn after surviving life's hardest situations. Floating is a state of trust. There's an element of confidence in it. It's the place we all long to live in, where we feel spacious, light, steady, clear, and free. But just like the other states of being, it's something we move in and out of, depending on what season we're in, what's happening around us, and how grounded we are inside ourselves.

Unlike the other states of being, Floating doesn't become a stereotype. It doesn't fracture into extremes or get distorted into dysfunctional behaviors. That's worth pausing over, because every other state included a spectrum, and a warning, of what can happen when those beautiful intentions get twisted. Overgiving becomes martyrdom. Receiving can tilt toward entitlement. Observing can slide into emotional detachment. But floating doesn't bend like that.

By definition, Floating resists distortion. It is presence without resistance. It doesn't cling, pretend, or perform. It isn't fragile or passive, and it doesn't collapse into fake serenity or bypass pain. It simply is. And that is what makes it so spiritually valuable.

When you are truly floating, you aren't striving to appear calm. You aren't acting like you've transcended life. You aren't faking peace to avoid conflict. You are surrendering, not into helplessness, but to buoyancy. You are allowing yourself to be held by something stronger than fear. That kind of release doesn't produce suffering. In fact, it's the opposite of suffering. It's the space without the grasping that suffering often comes from. It's like a resignation, a relinquishing, a letting go.

Every other extreme version of the states we've explored comes with a kind of self-selected suffering, a need, a regret, or a fear. But Floating exists outside of that pattern. It's not based on control, self-protection, proving, or earning.

We can't float without surrendering, and we can't fake floating. Try it the next time you're at a pool. Take a breath, go under, hold your knees and your breath, and let the water have its way with you. Don't fight or kick or tense up. Just allow yourself to become still, loose, more like the water itself. For some, it's not easy. It takes more courage than people realize. Letting go, even for a moment, is one of the bravest things we do. Floating invites a deep kind of inner permission. You don't float by accident. You float because you have chosen trust over fear, and that choice reminds you who you really are.

To live in this state, even briefly, requires a constellation of values. These are not just abstract virtues; they are lived truths, formed in grief, practiced in tension, and anchored in grace.

Humility. Floating is rooted in humility. Not the kind that shrinks, but the kind that stands quietly whole. Humility here means seeing yourself clearly: your strengths and limitations, your wisdom and wounds, without shame. There's no need to inflate or hide. Floating allows you to let others help. It's not weakness, it's trust. That creates space for intimacy and belonging.

Empathy. In this state, empathy is present, but it's grounded. You're not losing yourself in other people's pain. You're witnessing with compassion while staying rooted in your own clarity. This enhances giving and receiving alike. Instead of merging, you're finding a connection without experiencing the loss of yourself.

Reciprocation. Floating thrives on mutuality without a scoreboard. It's just the sacred rhythm of giving and receiving over time, without manipulation or control. Reciprocity in the Floating state is free of conditions. It's relational instead of transactional. The current moves both ways, and you trust the ebb and flow.

Vulnerability. Floating requires emotional courage. It invites us to release the armor and be seen, not because we need validation, but because we value honesty. Vulnerability here helps us become known, even when we feel exposed. That truth is what encourages others to be real, too.

Trust. You cannot float if you don't trust the water to hold you. The same is true in life. Trust here isn't naivety. It's discerned, chosen, and lived. It's the decision to believe that love still lives within people, and that we can BE the example of trustworthiness. That goodness still exists, and that we don't have to do this life alone. In fact, I think when we trust our inner knowing, it tells us we aren't meant to.

Faith. Floating is a deeply faithful posture. It's having a belief in spite of uncertainty, the unknown, or the mysterious. You may not have physical, tangible proof, but you know something real is holding you. Floating is living as if grace is real and love is foundational, even when nothing external has changed.

Generosity. Here, generosity isn't an effort. It flows. You're not trying to prove your goodness or overextend to feel worthiness. Generosity moves through you like breath. It creates warmth and builds trust. Nothing is forced in this state; it's free.

Self-Worth. Floating is impossible without deep self-worth. You are not trying to earn your place or build walls to protect yourself from need. You know who you are, even when you are quiet, not feeling particularly useful, and when your hands are open. Your value is unshakable.

Floating is stillness without feeling stuck and movement without struggle. This is the state of being where your soul has time to hear itself breathe. And no, we don't stay here forever. We're human, after all. We drift. But once we've known the water's hold and experienced the ease, we'll never forget it. We know how to come back here. And the next time love invites us to let go, we might just say yes and surrender to the flow within this state of Infinite Generosity.

Why Can't We Float?

So many people want to live in the Floating state. And why wouldn't they? It's light and peaceful. It's a place where you're not frantically trying to earn your worth, guard your heart, or fix everything around you. Floating is grace and trust. It's the version of you that has nothing left to prove and nothing left to fear.

But here's the question: *Is it possible to float when your world has been rocked?*

When tragedy strikes, when you're devastated, when everything you trusted has come undone, can you float?

I don't think we can. At least not at first. Floating isn't the first thing that comes. It's more like ebbing and flowing through all the emotions, and it doesn't look exactly the same for any of us. We're not floating when we're wrecked. Sometimes we're holding our breath, and sometimes we are hyperventilating. That's human, isn't it? That's real and honest.

Floating requires a certain kind of presence, an open softness. In the early days of pain, we don't have access to that. We are walking wounded, trying to make sense of chaos (so many replays and decisions) and willing the water to hold us up. But water doesn't work that way. This is what I keep coming back to: some people can't float because they're trying too hard.

In the water, the more you tense, the more you sink. It's personal, and it's physics. If you've ever taught someone to float, you've seen it. The moment they tighten up, lose faith in themselves, and stop trusting the water is the moment they start to sink.

And that sinking feeling is so, so scary. You know that feeling, right? It's a feeling like you are falling. And that is when, if you let it, the panic sets in. The brain/ego wants to get back in control, protect you, keep you safe and comfortable.

But it's the moment after the feeling of falling: if you can stick it out, holding your breath past the scary and terrifying, and by faith wait for the lift, it always comes. The water lifts you, rebalances you, and sets you up to be in a horizontal swimming position.

And then, it's up to you. You have the power to move forward or stand up and stop floating. Because floating isn't about forcing the water to hold you. You have to surrender to the water's nature. And if you're determined to stay in control, you're not going to float. You'll flail, struggle, and eventually wear yourself out. You will sink if you harden your body with tension.

People who can't float are often the ones who think they have to act upon the water. They believe it's their job to manipulate the laws of nature and make the water conform to their will. But water doesn't bend to our panic. It follows its own order, its own rules. The more you resist, the less compliant to your will it gets.

In spiritual terms, Floating asks us to become one with what holds us. Not to fight it or demand something different, but to move with it, and to say, "I will not resist the mercy that's trying to carry me today."

This is the practice. Learning to shift from "me versus the water" to "me in collaboration with the water." Us. Together. It's not me against life; it's me inside life. It's not me against the people I don't understand; it's me alongside them. That posture changes everything.

I remember reading Father Greg Boyle's book *Tattoos on the Heart* during this most painful season in my life. He talks about working with gang members in LA—people who have suffered more than most of us can imagine, people society has written off as irredeemable—and how the work is about creating belonging rather than trying to "fix" them.

Father Greg doesn't see broken people who need saving. He sees human beings who need to be seen. The gang members who walk through the doors of Homeboy Industries aren't projects, statistics, or cautionary tales. They're sons and brothers and fathers. They're people who've been told their whole lives that they don't matter, that they're disposable, that their mistakes define them forever.

But Father Greg creates an environment of "only us" instead of "us and them." He helps the world see past their tattoo-covered bodies, past their records and their reputations, to the truth of who they are: *us*. They are us. Not charity cases. Not the lucky recipients of our benevolence. Just us—flawed, trying, worthy of love.

That shattered me in the best way. Because if those men—who society deemed unredeemable—are us, then so am I. If they deserve mercy despite their worst moments, then maybe I do too. If belonging isn't something you earn through perfection but something you receive simply by being human, then maybe I still belong.

When I read it, I was deep in an us-and-them narrative with the Foundation that was not of my choosing. I was on the board of an organization called Voices for Children, and Father Boyle came to speak for an event we put on for childcare professionals. Here I was, sitting in the audience, listening to this man talk about radical inclusion, and I felt it like a lightning bolt: There is no them. There is only us.

I wasn't fully there yet. There was no cultivated "us" between me and Mitchell's family. No bridge. Nothing I had done, or not done, seemed to shift that. And I'm not going to take that on as my fault. But I also recognize that in that season of my life, I wasn't floating. I was still trying to make sense of the pain that didn't have a clean resolution. I didn't know whether to reach out or stay silent. I didn't know what could help to heal or just make things worse. And floating doesn't live in that kind of confusion.

So if you're asking yourself why you can't float, start here. Are you tensing? Are you fighting? Are you trying to control the water instead of becoming one with it? Are you making up a story and living like it's the truth? I am so guilty of all of these. And I have experienced the panic, the resistance, the pattern of thinking enough to recognize, finally, the rollercoaster ride I kept getting on.

You'll find yourself in the Floating state of being when you stop clenching your teeth and you unclasp your hands. It's the place where you finally let yourself be held. The truth of the matter is that sometimes, before you float, you sink. Not forever, but enough to learn that grace doesn't come through force.

There's no Floating without surrender. That's why we can't stay here all the time. It's not a stereotype or a posture we can mimic. We can't fake Floating. We're either resting in that infinite flow of universal love or we aren't.

When you're ready, you'll know. The water will feel different. Not because the water changed, but because you did.

Growing Your Faith in the Floating State

When I look back at that time in my life, I realize something simple and sacred: I didn't choose to float. I had to. There wasn't another option.

I had come to the end of what I could control and what I could carry. There is a moment of surrender here—Rob Bell reminded me that that is what God asks of us. To recognize and realize that we need Him. That we aren't meant to go it alone. I was defeated, exhausted, raw, and ill-equipped. He asks us to surrender it all. I could either keep fighting the current by pushing through and trying to keep it all together, or I could lift my feet off the floor and trust that something, someone, would hold me.

That's all I had to hold onto, ultimately. Faith. The raw kind that shows up when nothing else is working. The kind you grab hold of like a ladder in the dark when it is the only option other than despair.

Rose gave me a powerful image once. It came from her own season of painful uncertainty, when her husband's life hung in the balance and sleep felt impossible. She told me that on those sleepless nights, she would imagine herself curling up in the palm of Jesus's hand and resting there. Not escaping. Not solving. Just resting.

That image became a lifeline for me. A small, precious refuge I could retreat to when the noise in my head and the pain in my heart threatened to unravel me. I would close my eyes and picture it—His hand, warm and steady, holding me while I shook. Holding me while I wept. Holding me when I couldn't hold myself together anymore.

Eventually, I realized something: I had done it. Somewhere along the way, without even noticing, that tight ball of panic and dread I was carrying had uncurled. It had softened. It had found its way into His hand.

I wasn't always a follower of Jesus. I didn't have a neat spiritual path before the accident. I was raised Catholic, yes. But I'd been wandering spiritually for a long time, searching, visiting churches, hoping to find the right place to land. My husband, Don, came with me to Catholic Mass despite his Southern Baptist roots and his struggle with organized religion. He's a gentle, loving, steady man, but he couldn't be my spiritual anchor.

I felt the ache to find a community. And one day, I asked someone on my team where they went to church. They suggested St. Francis of Assisi.

And of course, it was St. Francis. How beautifully fitting. The saint who saw God in all of creation—in birds and wolves and water. Who preached that every living thing deserves reverence, that we're all part of the same sacred fabric. The patron saint of animals and ecology, yes, but also of peace. Of rebuilding what's been broken.

Here I was, someone who'd spent her life in the water, teaching people to trust it, to float in it, to let it hold them. And I was being led to a church named for the saint who called water "Sister Water"—humble, useful, precious, and pure. The saint who understood that creation itself teaches us how to love.

It felt like a gentle whisper: *You're exactly where you need to be.*

I walked into that church desperate for leadership, for guidance, presence, grounding, and for something ancient and steady. The first thing I saw was a table full of books. Right there in front of me was Matthew Kelly's *Rediscover Catholicism.* I had known him from the business world, having read *The Dream Manager*, his leadership book about building a great culture by helping team members identify and achieve their dreams. I picked up the book, started reading, and began attending Mass again. Slowly and intentionally, I started re-engaging with my faith.

But I was still losing it on the forty-five-minute drive to work. I would just dissolve in the car, crying the kind of cry that hijacks your body and doesn't let go. It was the daily coming-to-acceptance process. I would arrive at work with swollen eyes and a puffy face. I would sit in the car and gather my strength, barely able to pull it together, affixing a mask to my face to show up as the leader I had signed up to be.

So I started stopping by the tabernacle chapel at St. Francis, the little space where the Eucharist is kept for adoration and protection. I would sit there and pray, write, and cry. I had no outlet for my emotions. So many feelings I was containing to protect others, to carry the load, to be strong. Praying in my head wasn't working. I needed to write it all down, feverishly releasing it all on the page with the hope that comfort and clarity would find me in the aftermath. I needed to sit in something bigger than me. There was a big sign in that chapel: *Jesus, I trust in You.* The phrase became a lifeline. A friend of mine sent me a text during that time that simply said, "When you are overwhelmed and untethered, just say His name. That's enough. Just repeat again and again, 'Jesus.'"

That was all I could manage some days. Just this whisper of trust.

It occurred to me that if I was going to lean on God and put my trust in Him, I needed to start engaging with His words and direction. I wanted a relationship with God. I wanted to understand Him and what He wanted me to do with this terrible tragedy. I needed Him to help me survive the social media backlash and character assassination. And I was so grateful for all the incredible acts of love and support from so many wonderful people in my life. I felt like the greenest Catholic in the world. All I knew were the "rules" of Catholic worship and protocol. Things like not eating an hour before Mass, or never leaving Mass before the priest. There was very little actual spiritual instruction or opening.

I found a contemplative prayer group that welcomed me with open arms. They were reading Richard Rohr's book *The Divine Dance.* Richard Rohr is an incredible teacher and contemplative priest. His words helped me recognize that God is always with us, in us, for us, and He works through us. I was desperate for that collaboration.

Eventually, I joined a Bible study for the first time. And guess what book we studied? Wisdom. *Yes!* That's exactly what I was begging God for. Not clarity or outcomes, just wisdom. *Show me the way. Help me hear and heed You. How do I respond? What do I do now? Do I fight for my business, my reputation, my life's work? Do I stay silent in an effort to honor all the grief? Do I sell the business? Do I hold on tighter? I am scared. What is the right thing to do here?*

I found myself asking others what they thought I should do as ever-increasingly difficult situations presented themselves. And what I found was they didn't really know. No one in my life had experienced what I was facing. There were no roadmaps. My mentor encouraged me to sell the business, but I didn't have someone who could guide me through what was happening to me internally. I had to go ancient and turn to the God I loved as a child, who never left me.

So what does any of this have to do with Floating?

Everything.

Because floating in faith isn't some kind of passive, default setting. It's intentional, active surrender. This state is the practice of choosing love again and again, especially when nothing makes sense. I know that sounds so sappy, but I believe it to be true.

Floating means choosing to live with an open heart every day, orienting yourself toward Infinite Generosity even when everything in you wants to shut down. It's when you pause long enough to see someone and smile, choosing eye contact, engagement, and connection. You find yourself expanding instead of shrinking, and letting love lead your decisions instead of fear.

And yes, it's a practice. Some days, it's conscious and hard-won. Other days, it becomes unconscious and natural. The goal is to let love become our default and to move through life with generosity as our slant.

What's the Generous Thing to Choose Here?

When you are in the Floating state, the generous thing to do doesn't always look dramatic or visible. It can be quiet and internal. It often begins with one simple but sacred question:

How do I care for myself so I can show up for others?

That was the thread that ran through everything for me in that season, especially in my role as a leader. I wasn't floating because life was easy. I was floating because it wasn't. I was choosing it. And re-choosing it every day, relearning how to trust that I was held.

It didn't start from strength. It started from exhaustion, grief, and the understanding that I had no way to fix what happened. But I kept asking, *What's the generous thing to choose right now?* More often than not, the answer that came to me was: *Take care of yourself so you can take care of them.*

There's a kind of discipline to that, an emotional stewardship, if you will. It's a type of leadership grounded in humanity that feels sustainable.

I knew I had a company full of people who had stayed. Through the storm, the headlines, and all the uncertainty, my leaders didn't leave. My managers didn't leave. Sure, we lost a few sweet, nineteen-year-old front desk girls who understandably couldn't bear to pick up the phone anymore—not when every ring brought dread, not knowing if the voice on the other end would be kind or cruel. But the majority of our people stayed.

And so I had to ask myself, *Who do I need to be for them?*

The answer wasn't to be perfect. It wasn't holding it together at all costs. Instead, it was to be real. Be open. Be grounded.

That's why I stopped at church so often on my way to work. Not because I had extra time, but because I needed that pause to pour out myself, again and again. I needed that sacred breath between who I was at home in my despair and who I wanted to be when I walked through the doors of our schools. Those thirty minutes in the chapel were where I could dissolve into a puddle, and the mess could come out instead of getting pushed down.

Because here's what I learned: If you don't let the grief come out, if you try to smoosh it down, it'll squeeze out the sides, like the guts of a crushed cockroach. You can't press pain down forever. It leaks, it oozes, and it surprises you in the middle of staff meetings, grocery store aisles, and pick-up lines at school.

So the truly generous thing to do here is to let it come out somewhere. Create space for it—in therapy, in your journal, with a trusted friend, in prayer, on long drives where you can scream into the void. Process it intentionally, in a container you've chosen, so you don't end up unintentionally handing your unprocessed pain to the people who trust you to lead.

Because that's what happens when we don't create space for our grief and rage. It leaks out sideways. It shows up as impatience with a team member who asks the wrong question at the wrong time. As sharpness with a client who couldn't possibly know what you're carrying. As withdrawal from the people who need you present. They don't deserve to carry what you haven't processed. And you don't deserve to live with the shame of knowing you let it spill onto them.

But it isn't just them.

Everyone is a target for our stuffed-down rage, humiliation, and shame. I wasn't perfect. I was on a quest for healing, for wholeness, for forgiveness, for penance, for rectification, for grace and mercy. And I was on that quest partly because I saw the sadness in my husband's eyes. He was sure he was losing me.

My second therapist, Emily, who had a Yoda doll I hated on one of her chairs, encouraged me to feel my rage and release it. With her guidance, I went through my cabinets and drawers, stockpiling logoed coffee cups, chipped plates, and one-off glasses so that I could throw them at a wall in the garage and smash them in a safe place to release some pent-up steam. I found a Rage Room that had keyboards and monitors to smash with a sledgehammer or a bat. I screamed in my car with frustration and regret when the narrative got so far from the truth that I had to send a cease and desist letter.

I remember walking into our third location one Saturday morning. The energy was different, quieter. There were fewer families than we used to have. I wasn't doing anything big, just tidying up and straightening chairs, trying to stay present. And I walked past this one mom. She looked me straight in the eye, and I didn't say a word. But my tears just came, and I couldn't stop them. She immediately pulled me into a hug and let me cry.

That's generosity, too. Letting someone see you and hold you while you catch your breath. No pretending, just being real.

The generous thing can be as simple as choosing to be soft when your instinct is to harden, to be present when it would be easier to check out, or choosing to trust and lean in when fear is screaming at you to stay back and take cover.

In the Floating state, generosity feels like buoyancy, like being lifted as you lift others. There's no scorekeeping, no exhaustion from over-functioning. It's just love, flowing in and out of you, sustaining you as you go.

Questions to Ask Yourself

If you're in that place right now, trying to decide what the generous thing is, ask yourself:

1. Who do I want to be in the world?
2. What does it feel like when I am giving and receiving from love, and when am I giving from fear?
3. How am I allowing myself to be seen?
4. When can I make it a priority to care for myself so that I can care for others?
5. What is my outlet for grief to move through me so I don't keep stuffing it down?
6. How can I show up as the version of me that is most grounded in grace, mercy, and love?

CHAPTER SEVEN

Go with the Flow

There's a current running through my life's story. That current has carried me from childhood into leadership, from grief into grace, and from survival into surrender. It's the flow of giving and receiving. Of letting myself be loved by people and by God. Of choosing not to fight the water but to float in it.

I didn't know this was where the book would end when I started writing it. But now that we're here, it all seems so clear. I can see the moments that prepared me for what I didn't know was coming, and the people who showed up with generosity when I didn't even know what I needed or how to ask for it.

One of the most important gifts I received in life was swimming lessons. My mom never learned how to swim. She lost both her parents before she turned twenty—an only child who carried a sense of aloneness I didn't understand until I was older. But even without that skill herself, she made sure that her kids, all three of us, learned how to swim.

And not just doggy paddle. She made us summer-league swim-team-level swimmers. We spent our summers diving off blocks, perfecting our flip turns, racing the clock and each other. I think part of the reason she was so adamant about it was because she couldn't bear the thought of losing one of us to something as preventable as drowning.

She'd already lost too much. Swimming lessons were her way of protecting us from a fate she could control—even if she couldn't give us the gift of her own parents, even if she couldn't undo her own aloneness, she could give us this: the ability to save ourselves in the water.

And I loved it. I mean, I really loved it. I still do.

Starting at age five, swimming was my thing. I loved the instant quiet and peacefulness that occurred just under the surface. I found the water to be an incredible playground for testing what I didn't realize were science experiments. I can remember playing with my own buoyancy, challenging the laws of cause and effect, displacement, and gravity. I remember teaching myself to float by using the handrail on the stairs, and testing what happened when I held my breath, pulled myself down to the bottom of the pole, and then let it go.

I joined the YMCA year-round AAU swim team in the fall of 1973, and by the time I was ten, I was the Illinois state champion in the 50-yard breaststroke. I can still see the huge Ball State University bleachers suspended above the pool, and my parents front and center above my lane, cheering with pride and encouragement. Those are memories etched in joy. Swimming gave me something solid when life felt slippery or unpredictable. It gave me confidence, purpose, and peace. It was a gift I didn't even know I was receiving until much later. My sister and I became lifeguards and swimming instructors, and I became a summer league, novice, and high school swimming coach.

In my twenties, I became an entrepreneur. Sharing that love of swimming became a calling. And eventually, it became my business: Love to Swim School.

It was no small thing to build that first swim school location. We didn't have the assets to secure a loan to build the pool. Banks thought it was risky to finance two holes in the ground, understandably. But my mom (the same one who never learned to swim) chose to loan me the money, deep into her retirement. She gave me the start. She believed in what I was building, and she put it in writing. Hers wasn't just emotional support, but real financial investment. That moment, too, was giving and receiving.

That's how this has all unfolded. One generous offering at a time. A mother's vote of confidence. A coach's encouragement. My husband's commitment to us. Loans, letters, challenges, awards and opportunities, the grief, and a choice to fight for my story. And all of it has led me here.

That's why I say this isn't just a book. Infinite Generosity is a practice of noticing the truth when it rises in your body and being brave enough to respond to it.

Codie Sanchez talks about the tuning fork of truth. And the first time I heard her say it, something clicked. She said, "The truth is like a tuning fork; when we hear it, we feel it."[5] We all have this inner instrument that vibrates when something is true. You feel it in your body. Sometimes it's uncomfortable, especially when it asks something of you.

Here's the part we should come back to: We have to be present enough to notice it. This thing we are holding up to the light. Can we see it clearly? Objectively? Without emotion, judgement or obligation? What if it's not about you? What's it look like then?

We have to choose to pick it up, strike it, and listen. That isn't always easy when the world is loud, when our own pain is louder, and when other people's made-up stories start sounding truer than our own experiences.

And yet, this inner tuning fork, this inner knowing, is real. It's part of how God wired us to recognize what aligns with truth and what doesn't. Infinite Generosity is one of those truths. Whenever I share it, I see people lean in because they can feel it in their bodies. Generosity isn't scarcity, depletion, or performance. It's an infinity loop powered by humility and love. That's why it resonates.

I used to confuse truth with output. I thought worth came from overwork. I had an addiction to busyness, proving myself by achievement after achievement. It was a form of escape, believing I was only as worthy as my last accomplishment. That was the hum in my chest for years. But the tuning fork of God's wisdom struck a different note. His infinite wisdom and love guide me toward trust, faith, and love instead of choosing suffering.

One of the simplest ways that kind of clarity is described is in James 1:5: "If any of you lacks wisdom, let him ask of God, who gives generously to all without reproach, and it will be given to him." When the tuning fork hums, it's the Holy Spirit reminding us that wisdom is available, that we don't need to overcomplicate it or overexplain ourselves. We just need to ask, "Is this really true?" That question is a holy request for discernment. It creates space for peace, for forgiveness, for grace and mercy. When we are grounded in truth, it simply resonates.

When you feel that vibration of Infinite Generosity ringing in your chest, pay attention.

Sometimes, the generous thing to do is to take a breath. It can be telling the truth or staying silent. It can be surrendering to the outcome, and sometimes it's remembering where it all began: With a mother who didn't swim but made sure her daughter did. A daughter who didn't quit, even when the ground beneath her fell away in a moment. A community that held space. A God who never left.

The invitation is to go with the flow. To float in what is, rather than fight it. To let yourself be held, and to really listen for the sound of truth when it rings in your chest like a tuning fork. If you've felt it, you know exactly what I mean.

Take the Risk

When I think about what might make Infinite Generosity challenging for people to believe in or commit to, the first word that comes to mind is risk. Not just financial or material risk, though that can be a part of it. It's the emotional risk—the fear that if you give your time, energy, or presence, you might be taken advantage of. Or go unacknowledged, unreciprocated, or unvalued. Those fears are embodied in the stereotypes people have about giving and receiving.

The opposite of taking risks here would be choosing to honor yourself. This can also be uncomfortable, especially for people who have spent a lifetime being praised for how much they give. There's tension on both ends: giving too much or holding too tightly. Either way, you're confronted with discomfort.

My coach, Mike Kotsis, helped me see this differently. In our sessions, he used to take off his glasses and dramatically put them back on again while saying, "What if we looked at it through a different lens?" He did it so many times that I started reaching for my glasses when working with clients or even talking to myself. What would life be like if we looked through the lens of Infinite Generosity and applied it to everything?

It takes intentionality. You have to be willing to look again and ask yourself, "What are all the possibilities here? What version of this feels truest to me? Which one is most mutually honoring?" Mutuality is essential. We aren't giving so others can take. Or taking and then withholding.

I see it as a Namaste moment. God in me, honoring God in you. That's the heart of it.

For a long time, I used to walk around trying to breathe in Jesus and exhale myself. That was my practice. Breathing in that divine presence and trying to let His truest version of myself come through. I wanted to embody Him and abandon my shattered, grieving, sorrowful self. I wanted Jesus to take the wheel from my battered ego's hands, that constant voice in my head telling me lies as it fought to protect me. It wasn't easy. I had to work through so much resistance. That heavy, black winter coat I was carrying was hard to take off. I had to get honest about how I was actually hurting myself, even in my attempts to heal or be strong.

One moment that really shifted things for me happened during that same week in Denver. I was pointing out the life sentence of grief. Bemoaning the permanence of the empty chair at the dinner table, the empty bed in his room, and his empty car seat in the car. I carried the heaviness of knowing that this loss would never end. It could never be rectified or reversed. And my friend, Sara, looked me in the eyes and said, "I know that's not what you want for them. I know that's not what you're trying to attract to them, for them."

I was struck immediately with a realization. Sara was right. I wasn't trying to create suffering, but I was choosing it. I was playing that story on repeat so that I could hurt myself with the image of a grieving family, especially a grieving mother, whose suffering I thought I was accountable for and shared in. That realization helped me understand that my energy needed to shift. I wanted to choose what I sent out. If I kept rehearsing pain, I'd keep living in it. But if I could choose to send out love and stay open to a flow of mercy and grace, I could find more peace while intentionally putting God's love, grace, and mercy into the universe. That's what I wanted to create and perpetuate, not more impossible suffering weighing me down and keeping me small.

This realization doesn't mean life stopped being hard. As you know, life will still pull the rug out from under you. It could be a betrayal in a relationship, a death in the family, or a major loss in your business. It doesn't always have to be extreme to be hard. Sometimes, it's just the slow drip of everyday frustration or the daily grief that comes from loving deeply in a broken world.

You are going to keep moving, either by default or by intention. And if you've done this work by being honest with yourself, as you cultivated the foundation of Infinite Generosity, then you now have something deeper to tap into. You have new lenses to look through, or a tuning fork of truth to help you hear yourself, like Codie Sanchez describes.

Even with that inner knowing, fear still tries to get in. Fear of being judged, of rejection, of failing, of not being enough, or of giving too much. And then there's the mental spiral that follows with all the head trash and overthinking.

So the work becomes learning to override the voice of fear with your own intention. To ask, "What do I actually want to create here?" Not in some abstract future, but in this moment, during this conversation, or in this relationship. And are you willing to do it scared? That's the question that keeps showing up for me. Am I willing to live generously even when I'm afraid, don't know how it will be received, or when it's uncomfortable? I wrote this book scared. And I pray it is a beautiful act of generosity and love. That's my intention. To make something beautiful out of all this pain and suffering. To honor God's gift with this story and discovery.

There's no arrival point with Infinite Generosity. No one gets to perfect it. There are just these opportunities to practice. Again and again. And when you find yourself at a crossroads, you get to ask yourself, "Now, what do I want to create? Who am I going to be in the world?" In that pause, you get to choose.

This Is Bigger Than Me

I came across an interview where Anderson Cooper was interviewing Stephen Colbert. They were talking about grief, and Stephen said, "You have to learn to love the thing you most wish had not happened." I'd never heard of grief put quite like that. And then he went on to gently ask, "What punishments of God are not gifts?"

Anderson was visibly moved as he asked, "Do you really believe that?"

Colbert answered, "Yes. It's a gift to exist. And with existence comes suffering. There is no escaping that."[6]

He explained that if we're grateful for our lives, then we have to be grateful for all of it, even the parts we would never choose again. Colbert reminded me that suffering doesn't just harm us; it can expand us. He said it creates the awareness we need to connect with others, to love more deeply, and to see what it means to be human. It's the pulse of human experience that helps us realize that grief, loss, and longing can break our isolation and invite us into connection.

Colbert, who is Catholic and whose childhood grief was the loss of his two older brothers and his father in a plane crash at age ten, offered a kind of permission in that grief. His perspective isn't theoretical; it's real. It didn't offer me a quick fix, but it did make space for more honesty, vulnerability, and the faith that loss doesn't have to be wasted.

Consider that tension. We can sit with gratitude and heartbreak together. We can believe that something wounded can still be held, and that even the pieces of us that hold the most devastating scars can teach us something about what it means to love more truly and live more generously.

Why did I need to write this book? Because God gave this to me.

I had only one moment, in the first days after the accident, where the question of *Why* began to creep in. I remember it like it was yesterday. I am standing in my primary bathroom, forcing myself to get dressed, and the thought starts, *Why, Lord?* As soon as it formed, it dissolved.

DO NOT ASK WHY, a voice said loudly in my head. The voice asked more quietly, *Why not you?*

And so the question became, *What do You want me to do with this, Lord?* How do I respond to a calling that I didn't ask for but couldn't ignore? This book came from searing pain, unexpected joy, vulnerable inspiration, and endless prayers. It came from moments of deep silence when I didn't have answers, and moments of clarity that only came after long seasons of confusion.

It came because someone looked me in the eyes and said, "Thank you for your suffering and experience. I honor the journey you've been on for us. Help us now. You've been stuck in your pain, your suffering. But we need the learning. Share with us what you've learned." Those words undid me and built me back up all at once. I realized that my story mattered, not just in the living of it, but in the telling of it. That my grief and pain mattered. That my voice had weight. That my truth was sacred.

So many times, people quoted James 1:2–4 to me: "When troubles of any kind come your way, consider it an opportunity for great joy. For you know when your faith is tested, your endurance is fully developed, you will be perfect and complete, needing nothing." Consider it all joy, they said to me again and again. *Wow, Lord*, I thought to myself. *Tough ask.* And yet here I am, collecting my blessings and sharing my story with you.

I want to say that to you, too. Your story matters, too.

This book is an act of love, honor, faith, and generosity. It's a living testimony to what it means to keep going, to stay with the questions, to lead when you're unsure, and to give from a place that's been emptied and refilled over and over again. I wrote it because I want to live energetically from love as much as I possibly can. And maybe, just maybe, this book helps you do that too.

I've learned that generosity is really just love in action. Not just a feeling, not a label, but a way of being that shows up in the room, in our decisions, and in the way we speak to ourselves and others. Jesus called us to love in action, even and especially in our suffering. I've learned that it's possible. I won't say it's easy, but it's possible.

One of the themes that has stuck with me during the writing of this book is the idea of nobility. What does it mean to act with nobility, especially when you aren't sure what the "right" thing is? There were so many moments I didn't know what to do. Should I go to the hospital? Should I fire everyone involved? Do I temporarily close this location, and if I do, when and how do I reopen? Do I stand up for myself and the business, or do I stay quiet in an effort to do no additional harm? These weren't theoretical decisions. They were real and urgent. And yet, even in the mess, I kept coming back to that inner knowing. I may not know the perfect answer, but I can show up with integrity. I can choose the most generous action available to me at the moment. I can choose nobility.

And for those who want to think deeply about the roots of this way of being, there's a reason C. S. Lewis asked whether Jesus was a lunatic, a liar, or Lord. It matters how we see Him. When I look at His life, I see a model of infinite generosity. If I'm going to say I follow Him, then I need to reflect that generosity in my own life.

So here's what I've come to believe: We get to create what we want in this life. Yes, it takes courage and discernment and a lot of starting over, but ultimately, I know what we all want is to love and be loved. I know that to be true. And living a life of Infinite Generosity is one of the clearest paths I know to that mutual love.

For me, intention and action are imperative. When I lead with love, when I stop to ask my heart what it really wants, when I pause in prayer to listen to Jesus or the Divine in me, I become more compassionate, generous, grounded, open, and real.

I've also learned that I cannot control everything. Believe me, I've tried. But in every scenario, even the ones that brought me to my knees, I can say this: I always did my best. That's it. That's all anyone can ask of us. And when we act from that place, there's no shame, just grace and growth.

I've seen Infinite Generosity play out most practically in my work as an EOS Implementer®. I see it when leaders and managers grow because they've committed to growing their people. I see it in tools like Delegate and Elevate™, where the system supports not just getting things done, but doing it in a way that lifts others up and helps them become more and better. I see it in the way I get to show up in the room with openness, honesty, objectivity, and compassion.

This is the gift of living inside Infinite Generosity. Instead of striving to be perfect, we can choose to be available. We can love, lead, live with courage, and stay soft when the world hardens around us. It means showing up anyway, putting yourself in the current, and going with the flow.

Keep Going

What does it mean to flow with Infinite Generosity? It's an act of faith amidst our human imperfection. It doesn't always look graceful or feel good, but there is peace here. That's what I've found. When I live from this place of staying conscious, open, soft, and strong, there's less self-selected suffering. There's more connection. And more connection means a richer, more meaningful existence. Infinite Generosity is having a bias for loving and being loved.

When I drift from it, I've learned how to find my way back. The core belief that helps me return is this: I have a choice. That's the hinge.

I first learned it in high school when I read *Man's Search for Meaning* by Viktor Frankl, a Holocaust survivor who endured the unthinkable and still found meaning and love in his suffering. He said, "Everything can be taken from a man but one thing: the last of the human freedoms—to choose one's attitude in any given set of circumstances, to choose one's own way."[7] I carried that truth nugget in my soul like a little charm in my pocket.

I had a teacher, Dr. Davies, who had studied to be a Jesuit priest. We'd meet in the chapel at Culver, the college prep school I attended in Indiana, and he taught me how to say the rosary. It's a prayer offered to Mother Mary, in contemplation of the life of Christ. I didn't know it then, but I was learning how to anchor myself. How to return. How to choose.

Then, in my Bible study group, I started learning how to stay, how to be present, and how to hold what was true without trying to control or fix it all. I learned that faith has to transcend reason. We can't intellectualize everything into a satisfying little package. Some things defy language. Some things are mysteries and always will be.

No one could have told me any of that at the beginning of my journey. I don't think anyone could have said the "right" thing or told me the right thing to do. I was in brand-new territory—not just for me, but for most of the people around me. I had a few close friends who'd gone through similarly traumatic business experiences. But they had lived through it in a different time, before the cancel culture of social media.

So I had to learn how to come back to myself. And in doing so, I found my way back to generosity.

This whole book has been an exploration of that. What it looks like to live generously as a way of being. The only way to be a part of Infinite Generosity is to practice it. Test it out on your life. Let yourself be more present to the possibilities.

Don't try to get it right.

Instead, let's ask ourselves, "What's the generous thing to choose here? What resonates with me?" Let's allow ourselves to be curious and open to the opportunities that help us return to love.

Even when we're closed off.

Even when we're feeling small, or bitter, or scared.

Even when we've failed to live it out.

We can always return. That's the most generous truth of all.

A Full-Circle Moment

My friend Krisana, who owns Spanish immersion preschools, reached out to me one day. She told me about a tragic accident at a Montessori school in town. A parent in the 4:00 p.m. pick up line got her children in her car, and then accidentally compressed her accelerator hard. Her car pushed the one in front of her, and then both cars went over the curb and through an iron fence where a teacher was supervising children playing. They were pinned under the car and the fence. The twenty-two-year-old teacher and a fourteen-month-old child died. Four other children were injured. A lawsuit was filed against the driver and also included the Montessori School.

Knowing my story, Krisana asked if I would reach out to the owner and offer my support. She saw that maybe I could be someone who could help him navigate the unthinkable. Her call touched me. It felt like one of those full-circle moments where the pain of my experience could help me help someone else. That made me grateful, because being able to sit with him in his devastation gave some purpose to my own.

When I dialed the phone, I didn't prepare a script or even really think much about what wisdom I could offer. I simply committed to being present with him and listening. Sometimes, what we need most is someone who can relate, who has an idea of what we are going through, especially when very few people in the world can.

The owner was raw, devastated, and overwhelmed. He told me about the lawsuit he was facing. He talked about the tidal wave of voices on the internet, all of the Monday morning quarterbacks with strong opinions of what should have been done to prevent such a tragedy. There was a lot of public outrage and finger-pointing. Some of it came from an understandable desire to make sure it never happens again. But for him, in the middle of grief, the weight of that righteousness made it all the harder to breathe.

At one point, he asked me what I would do. I shared some of my own regret, not as prescriptions for him, but as data points for him to consider as he made his decisions. I told him that one of my deepest regrets was not standing up for myself more publicly. I wished I had said more openly how devastated we were, how profoundly sorry we were, and how truly accidental it all was. I carried that silence as a weight, and I did not want him to carry the same.

I also encouraged him to listen to his gut. Our brains are beautiful and powerful, but they are only cerebral. When we let our brains drive everything, we can miss the wisdom that comes from deeper within us. I told him to drop into his heart, to listen to his stomach, and to give those places equal time alongside his thoughts. Balanced decisions do not come from logic alone. They come from allowing your whole self to weigh in: your mind, your heart, and your soul.

He thanked me for our conversation. For me, the gift was being able to show up for him. Infinite Generosity is like that. We don't have to solve or fix anything. We don't have to come up with all the right words or provide perfect answers. But we do get to see love flowing in both directions. In that moment, love and humility intersect. There is no judgment or attachment to an outcome. Instead, we find openness, vulnerability, and one human heart reaching toward another.

That is Infinite Generosity in practice: to give of ourselves with no expectation of what will come back, unattached to the outcome, and to receive with gratitude when love flows back to us. That day reminded me that sometimes the most generous thing we can offer is our presence and our willingness to sit in the fire with someone who feels very much alone and just listen to them.

Final Thoughts

As we come to the end of this book, one realization has settled deep into my soul: You don't need to love me for me to love you. Love is not a transaction or a bargain that needs to be struck. It isn't conditional upon being returned in equal measure. Love, in its truest and most generous form, is a choice. And that means I am free to love you anyway, and in any way I choose.

That freedom is at the heart of Infinite Generosity. It reshapes the question we ask when life brings us face to face with conflict, loss, or even simple misunderstanding. Instead of asking, "How do I get what I need here?" or "How do I protect myself?" Infinite Generosity invites us to pause and ask, "How can I love you?" In this moment, given this situation and who we both are right now, what is the loving choice that honors us both?

It doesn't mean the answer will always be easy. Sometimes, the most generous thing to do is to set a boundary. Sometimes, it's choosing silence, forgiveness, or walking away with peace.

I have learned that love expressed through generosity is never wasted. Even when it isn't received the way I hoped, when it goes unnoticed, or when it costs me something. If it is grounded in humility and offered in truth, it carries weight. It attracts peace.

It changes the atmosphere. It changes us.

I want to say this: I am thankful. Deeply, soulfully, awefully thankful. For every person, conversation, hardship, and joy that has brought us to this moment. I wouldn't be who I am, nor could I have written these words, without all of those threads weaving me together.

My prayer is that something here has stirred your own tuning fork of truth, that you have felt the resonance of Infinite Generosity calling you into a deeper way of being.

Wherever you go from here, whatever challenges or opportunities await, may you carry this question with you: ***What is the generous thing to choose here?*** If you ask it faithfully, you will find your way. It may not be perfect, but it will be filled with more peace, clarity, and love.

All you can do is your very best. That's all anyone can do. And that is enough. More than enough.

If you can keep your head when all about you
    Are losing theirs and blaming it on you,
If you can trust yourself when all men doubt you,
    But make allowance for their doubting too;
If you can wait and not be tired by waiting,
    Or being lied about, don't deal in lies,
Or being hated, don't give way to hating,
    And yet don't look too good, nor talk too wise:

If you can dream—and not make dreams your master;
    If you can think—and not make thoughts your aim;
If you can meet with Triumph and Disaster
    And treat those two impostors just the same;
If you can bear to hear the truth you've spoken
    Twisted by knaves to make a trap for fools,
Or watch the things you gave your life to, broken,
    And stoop and build 'em up with worn-out tools:

If you can make one heap of all your winnings
    And risk it on one turn of pitch-and-toss,
And lose, and start again at your beginnings
    And never breathe a word about your loss;
If you can force your heart and nerve and sinew

To serve your turn long after they are gone,
And so hold on when there is nothing in you
   Except the Will which says to them: 'Hold on!'

If you can talk with crowds and keep your virtue,
   Or walk with Kings—nor lose the common touch,
If neither foes nor loving friends can hurt you,
   If all men count with you, but none too much;
If you can fill the unforgiving minute
   With sixty seconds' worth of distance run,
Yours is the Earth and everything that's in it,
   And—which is more—you'll be a Man, my son!

Rudyard Kipling

My husband, "Coach Don," coaching infant/toddler swimming during a class at the school.

My daughter, Reilly, Reilly celebrating a swimmer's progress with a high-five at the pool.

From left to right: me, my son Donovan, my husband Don, and Melissa—Don's daughter and our Sales Leader who started with us in 2005.

Speaking at the USSSA conference on February 10, 2018, prior to the call that would change everything and split my life into a before and after.

Hiking with Mary's Tribe, friends who walked beside me through heartbreak and healing.

The quilt made from swim school T-shirts across the country, organized by Casie Shore and delivered by Tammy Schoen.

Acknowledgements

First and foremost, I want to thank God. Believe me, nearly eight years ago as I write this now, I never would have seen how I could be grateful to God for this terrible, preventable accident. But the truth is, He was my refuge, my guide, my soulmate in suffering, my comfort. He is always my guide when I choose generosity.

I was blessed to be surrounded by my best friends when I got the call. And then, so many people came forward to love me. Most immediately, Rose Cholewinski, Miren Oca, Jim Spiers, David Gorman, Don Maranca, Melanie Kirk, and Mario Ochoa (RIP) were among the first responders in the early days and weeks after the accident. Kendra Walker was with me, Rose, and Miren at dinner that night. I was surrounded by strength. I knew they were in it with me.

To my extraordinary Girl's Trip Tribe: Rose Cholewinski, Kendra Walker, Miren Oca, Micha Seal, Kathy Hubbard, Ann Marie Sunderhaus, and Karen Clay, your compassion, support, and encouragement made this book possible. Thank you for loving me. It is my honor to be loved by you.

To my incredible Entrepreneur's Organization (EO) San Antonio Forum mates: Russell Reyes, Magaly Chocano, John Malfer, Harvinder Singh, Melody Zamora, Heather Tessmer, Charissa Cardinal, thank you for all you did to help me and love me. Your friendship and support, your willingness to listen to me process my pain and watch me cry for years and years, I know it wasn't easy. Thank you for your advice, encouragement, love, and guidance. I am a better human because of all of you.

Thank you to my truly special friends on my TAB (short for The Alternative Board) Board: Don Maranca, Steve Kramer, Kay Scoggins, John Lujan, Alfredo Avalos, Brent Statzer, Juan Carlos Almanza, George Salinas, Neilesh Verma, and Michael Rodriguez. My rockstar friends. Your compassion, love, support, and friendship have made such an impact on my life, and who I am, and who I want to be in the world. Thank you so much for everything. I love you all. And Don, your generous support, belief, care, accountability, questions, and friendship are gifts I will keep sacred for the rest of my life.

Who would I be if I didn't shout out my Book Club peeps: Carrie DeMont, Buffy Folise, Ann Marie Sunderhaus, David Gorman, Karen Clay, Melissa Taylor, Miren Oca, Rose Cholewinski, and Krissy Bartlett. I love you people. This club was a COVID creation and became a life raft for all of us over the years. You were and are such an important tether for me. Thank you for your commitment to growth, greatness, and connection. I am more and better because of you.

As I pursued help and healing, I was blessed to find so many healers and helpers. Emily Sanderson, thank you. You helped me learn how to release my anger and frustration in healthy, effective ways. Anne Seay, you are a goddess. You were such a light house and a mirror for me. Thank you doesn't even touch it. My heart is full of gratitude for the work you did and are doing in my life. Mike Kotsis, you are a reason my faith is so strong. God and I were just talking about who I might need next in my journey to becoming whole again. And then, you dropped out of the sky, sitting at my table randomly at a QCE cocktail hour. Wow. How fortuitous. You were the link in the chain I needed to come back to myself. Thank you, Coach Mike. I am your friend forever.

To my Denver Journey group, thank you for the breakthrough, encouragement, compassion, true generosity in action, physical presence, parades, speeches at parades, and the endlessness of possibility, Oneness, and creation. I love you forever, Love Monsters.

I knew I would need the help of a great team to take my discovery and story and turn it into something beautiful to share. The expert guidance and tender loving care that was taken to weave this story and Infinite Generosity together was magical and at times, quite difficult. Thank you to everyone who played a role in making this book possible. Jesse Barnett, Tracy Jenkins, and Andrew Biernat, I will be forever grateful for your patience, support, curiosity, and insight. You turned my pain into something I pray will help a lot of people. Jenifer Truitt and Karla Dial, thank you for your commitment to excellence and your willingness to duke it out with me for the greater good. It was fun working with you.

I want to acknowledge and appreciate every single person who ever believed in Love to Swim School's mission enough to work there. I pray your memories are warm and rewarding. I had so much fun growing our leadership with you. That includes my Love to Tumble people, too. I learned so much from you all. Thank you for being a great childhood learning experience and a positive memory for so many children and families. I intend to honor you with this book. I hope that's what you feel.

A very special shout-out to Melissa Magee, my bonus daughter and dear friend, who also worked her butt off helping to make Love to Swim School a success over 20 years. Thank you, Melissa, for everything. I love you.

I want to thank the entire U.S. Swim School Association, and especially Liza Zarda and Tracy Koleber, who allowed me to come back to our incredible learn to swim business community and hopefully, contribute meaningfully.

An eternal, reverberating thanks to the incredible swim school business friends who sent me, my family, or one of my swim school location teams something, some demonstration of love and support, for a year. Your belief in me, your support and compassion, it meant then and still means now, the world to me: Leslie Daland, Margee Charron, Pat Sunderhaus, Bob Hubbard, Cindy and Johnny Johnson, Lynn Ledford, Georgette Cutler, Dan Berzansky, Tammy Schoen, Buffy Folise, Rob Jacobsen, Mark Mahoney, Girls's Trip peeps and Book Club friends and so many, many more beautiful people from the US Swim School Association membership. It is an honor to know you and support the essential work of learn to swim and water safety education with you.

I want to acknowledge and thank my EOS Implementer Wise Women Group: Andrea Jones, Sandi Mitchell, Beth Fahey, Sara Stern, Barb Reimbold, Jackie Kibler, Monica Justice, Beth Berman, Tania Bengtsson, Shelley Woodrow, Megan Piper, Laura Rerucha, Mari Tautimes, and Lisa Gonzalez who have no idea how much inspiration and validation I have received from them. It's an honor and a privilege to know you, Ladies, and to call you my friends and colleagues.

Thank you, Jill Young, for having the courage to create connectedness between us all. Just that tiny bit of inspiration on your part keeps reverberating positively into the world. Thank you so much for your magical heart and inspiration.

Special shout-out to Mari Tautimes, whose generous vulnerability and skill in storytelling at that first retreat in San Diego inspired the courage in me to share this story here. Also, a special loving and honoring hug to Sara and Andrea. Your friendship is so special to me. Thank you for endless grace, mercy, love, discovery, possibility, expansion, and wondering. You are beautiful mirrors for me. I cherish the ways you help me see the divine in you, myself, and others.

To Kevin Moore, my dear, beautiful friend. There are very few people who have seen me at my most real and raw. You may never know how important your friendship is to me. Thank you for your example of patience, grace, and humility. And for being a constant support as I searched for wholeness. Thank you for loving me through so much.

To George Block, my long-time mentor, thank you. I was just a 19-year-old kid when I showed up to get certified as a lifeguard and then work at Northside Aquatics in 1986. I learned so much from you, George. Thank you for stepping up for me when I really needed someone to help me see a path and a perspective.

To Gino Wickman, EOS Worldwide, and the EOS Implementer community: Oh, to do such meaningful work with such amazing people! What a gift it is to be a part of it. Thank you for your part in making this book possible. You fortified me. You inspired me. You showed me myself and what is possible in the service of a greater good. I am afraid to even start naming people because I will leave someone out. I must call out Jim Coyle, Don Tinney, Don Maranca, Jill Young, Beth Fahey, Mighty CJ Dube', Sean O'Driscoll, Mike Paton, my August 2019 Detroit Boot Campers, Justin Maust, to name just a few of you who made me want to pursue greatness in the likeness of you. Thank you so much.

Derrick Smith, check it out! I stepped out of the boat! Thank you for your thoughtful kindness and encouragement. You made a mark on me.

To the EO San Antonio Board of Directors 2020-2023, thank you for allowing me to serve alongside you. I grew a lot in these years, and it fortified the foundation I get to stand on now. I am grateful for our parts in each other's stories.

To Tom Cuthbert and my Vistage Trusted Advisors group, thank you so much for welcoming me into your fold. You gave me inspiration, perspective, focus, encouragement, and community as I stepped further back into the flow. I learn so much from you. Some of my courage to release this book comes from you.

To every client who said yes to my EOS Implementer journey and to every client who said no, thank you for the experience and the learning. I have grown so much because of you. You are the inspiration for this book, ultimately. I pray it serves the people who need its message.

To Megan Shiver, thank you for your compassion and support throughout this process. How amazing it is that we found each other.

To my very best friend in the world, Rose Cholewinski, I love living life with you! You know my heart. Yes, we are on for our Saturday morning call.

To my children, Reilly and Donovan, I love living life with you! I learned the most about Infinite Generosity through my relationship with you. Thank you for being mine. I love you so much.

To my very best boyfriend in the world, Don Magee, I love living life with you! I will never stop marveling at the blessing we are to each other and how much God must love us to bring us together as spouses, partners, and friends. The odds were so against us. And look at us now. My rock. My safe place to land. I love you so much. Thank you for everything, My Love.

About the Author

As an entrepreneurial kid, Mary took advantage of a multitude of opportunities to "do business" with people. The funniest one was selling pictures of Charlie's Angels to the boys in her fourth-grade class. Mary grew up to be a 10th grade English teacher and high school swimming and water polo coach. But the entrepreneurial bug was in her, and she found herself building a learn-to-swim business from scratch, growing it to three year-round, indoor, stand-alone locations employing about 100 people at its peak. Mary sold that business in 2018.

In 2019, she committed to becoming an EOS Implementer so that she could help smart, challenged, growth-oriented companies install the Entrepreneurial Operating System (EOS) into their businesses.

Mary joined EO in 2012 while running her learn-to-swim business. She is a proud EO San Antonio member and has served the organization as a learning chair (2020 – 2022) and as a President (2022 - 2023). She achieved Expert EOS Implementer® status (500+ full day sessions) in June of 2025 and is currently serving as a Coach Contributor for the EOS Implementer® community. She cherishes the friendships and business contacts she has made through EO, many of whom have become EOS clients. Mary has a huge heart for entrepreneurial business owners and loves to see them succeed.

Connect with Mary

E-mail: mary@seewhatlovecando.com

Social media: linkedin.com/in/mary-reilly-magee-41997516

Website: SeeWhatLoveCanDo.com

Resources

Want to keep going? Here are the books, podcasts, and apps that guided me on this journey. If you're curious about where these ideas came from—or just want more to explore—dig in.

BOOKS

- Boyle, Gregory. *Tattoos on the Heart: The Power of Boundless Compassion*
- Brown, Brené. *Atlas of the Heart*
- Brown, Brené. *Braving the Wilderness*
- Brown, Brené. *The Gifts of Imperfection*
- Cameron, Julia. *The Artist's Way*
- Chandler, Steve. *Crazy Good: A Book of Choices*
- Chandler, Steve. *Creator*
- Cron, Ian Morgan and Suzanne Stabile. *The Road Back to You*
- Eldredge, John. *Beautiful Outlaw*
- Gilbert, Elizabeth. *Big Magic: Creative Living Beyond Fear*

- Gottlieb, Lori. *Maybe You Should Talk to Someone*
- Haig, Matt. *The Comfort Book*
- Hansen, Brant. *Unoffendable*
- Hardison, Amy and Alan D. Thompson. *The Ultimate Coach*
- Hardison, Amy. *The Ultimate Coach Concentrated*
- Holiday, Ryan. *Courage is Calling*
- Holiday, Ryan. *Discipline is Destiny*
- Holiday, Ryan. *Ego is the Enemy*
- Holiday, Ryan. *Right Thing, Right Now*
- Holiday, Ryan. *Stillness is the Key*
- Holiday, Ryan. *The Obstacle is the Way: The Timeless Art of Turning Trials into Triumph*
- Jaouad, Suleika. *Between Two Kingdoms*
- Katie, Byron. *Loving What Is*
- Kelly, Matthew. *Decision Point*
- Kelly, Matthew. *Life is Messy*
- Kelly, Matthew. *Rediscover Catholicism*
- Kelly, Matthew. *Rediscover Jesus*
- Kidd, Sue Monk. *The Book of Longings*
- Kidd, Sue Monk. *When the Heart Waits*
- Lencioni, Patrick. *The Three Signs of a Miserable Job*
- Lucado, Max. *You Are Special*
- Nepo, Mark. *The Book of Awakening*
- Pasricha, Neil. *The Happiness Equation*
- Rohr, Richard. *The Divine Dance: The Trinity and Your Transformation*
- Ruiz, Don Miguel. *The Four Agreements*

- Schein, Edgar H. and Peter A. Schein. *Humble Inquiry: The Gentle Art of Asking Instead of Telling*
- Singer, Michael. *Living Untethered*
- Singer, Michael. *The Untethered Soul*
- Tate, Christie. *Group: How One Therapist and a Circle of Strangers Saved My Life*
- Yamada, Kobi. *What Do You Do With a Problem?*
- Young, Sarah. *Jesus Calling*
- Bell, Rob. *Love Wins*
- Bell, Rob. *What We Talk About When We Talk About God*
- Bell, Rob. *What is the Bible?: How An Ancient Library of Poems, Letters, and Stories Can Transform the Way You Think and Feel About Everything*

PODCASTS

- *A Bit of Optimism* by Simon Sinek (two particular episodes: "A Lot of Optimism (Or The One Where I Met Andy Grammer)" and "Moving Forward with my sister Sara")
- *At Home* with Byron Katie
- *Eternal Life* by Rory Vaden
- *How I Built This* with Guy Raz
- *It's A Good Life* by Brian Buffini
- *Sunday Homilies* with Father Mike Schmitz
- *The Bible in a Year* with Father Mike Schmitz

- *The Daily Stoic* by Ryan Holiday
- *The RobCast* by Rob Bell
- *Unlocking Us* by Brené Brown

APPS

- Hallow
- Ascension
- Headspace
- The Work App with Byron Katie
- Daily Stoic

Notes

1 Dan Sullivan and Dr. Benjamin Benjamin Hardy, The Gap and the Gain: The High Achievers' Guide to Happiness, Confidence, and Success (Carlsbad, CA: Hay House Business, 2021).

2 Gregg Alexander and Rick Nowels, "New Radicals–You Get What You Give Lyrics," Genius.com, accessed November 24, 2025, https://genius.com/New-radicals-you-get-what-you-give-lyrics.

3 EOS stands for Entrepreneurial Operating System. Learn more at EOSworldwide.com.

4 Elizabeth Gilbert, "Letters from Love—with Special Guest Adam Skolnick,!" Letters from Love with Elizabeth Gilbert (Substack), October 5, 2025, https://elizabethgilbert.substack.com/p/letters-from-love-with-special-guest-8cd.

5 Codie Sanchez, "The REAL Truth About Getting Rich! ('I WISH Someone Had Told Me This Earlier!')," video uploaded by Lewis Howes, YouTube, posted October 14, 2024, https://www.youtube.com/watch?v=vehuPSifJ1s.

6 Anderson Cooper and Stephen Colbert, "Stephen Colbert and Anderson Cooper's Beautiful Conversation About Grief," uploaded by Mostly Water, YouTube, posted August 17, 2019, https://www.youtube.com/watch?v=YB46h1koicQ.

7 Viktor E. Frankl, Man's Search for Meaning (Boston, MA: Beacon Press), 2006.

www.ingramcontent.com/pod-product-compliance
Lightning Source LLC
LaVergne TN
LVHW020430070526
838199LV00025B/587/J